N 0025762 1

Local History and the Teacher

Local History and the Teacher

Robert Douch M.A.

Lecturer in Local History
University of Southampton Institute of Education

London: Routledge & Kegan Paul

First published 1967
by Routledge and Kegan Paul Ltd
Broadway House, 68-74 Carter Lane
London, E.C.4.

Printed in Great Britain
by Northumberland Press Ltd
Gateshead

Contents

Preface

The study of local history has become very popular in England in recent years. This increased interest has encouraged, and to some extent has been encouraged by, developments which have taken place in the use of local history at different levels of formal education.

Many teachers have long appreciated the important contribution which local history can make to education, but, since 1945, its virtues have been increasingly extolled to both members of, and entrants to, the profession. For example, a stream of books and articles has urged practising teachers to introduce local history into their work in school. Some of the most marked, and potentially most significant changes, however, have taken place in colleges of education. Today, in lecture courses, group projects and individual essays, many student teachers, both history specialists and others, investigate historical aspects of a local environment. Some such work may be immediately valuable to them as a part of their own specialised or general education: other activities will be designed to illustrate profitable ways in which local history can be used in school with children of different ages and abilities.

However convinced students and teachers may be of the value of local history, they soon realise that there are many difficulties associated with work in this field. Sometimes they have been warned of these before undertaking an investigation or teaching project: too often they have been left, unsuspecting, to discover the problems for themselves as work has proceeded.

The purpose of this book is to consider both the opportunities and the difficulties which the study and teaching of historical aspects of the local environment present, particularly in English teacher-training establishments and junior and secondary schools. Much of the contents should also be useful to students of local history generally and to teachers who are interested in environmental studies wherever, and at whatever level, they may be working.

The meaning of 'local' history may, of course, vary with, for example, the age and ability of pupils and the nature of topics studied. Here 'local' normally connotes the near neighbourhood of the college or school itself which the student or pupil already knows at first-hand or which can be brought within his experience in the course of the local work which is being carried out. Environments away from school or college obviously also lend themselves to 'local' study where a teacher thinks that such work is possible and desirable. Except where the context obviously implies a student-teacher, the word 'student' is used to mean anyone who is interested in studying a topic.

In Part I the development and value of local history studies in the work of English schools are considered. The very varied sources of local history are then discussed in Part II. The method of treatment adopted in describing particular types of sources varies according to the nature of the source and the knowledge of it which the student or teacher is likely already to possess. But always the character and content of the source-type are considered and practical suggestions given for finding out more about it, both generally and in relation to a specific locality. This second part normally takes the form of annotated lists of books and addresses, but it is supplemented, where necessary, with information about maps and pictorial records. The two sections have been kept separate so that readers may have unbroken narrative introductions and reference lists to the different types of material. The only chapters in which this pattern is not followed are those on 'Books' and 'Archives' where the accounts of printed works, repositories and classes of records would become unnecessarily complicated if the references were placed at the end. Considerable detail is included in each chapter, not because every student or teacher will need it all, but to enable individuals to select some sources and references which are relevant to their particular needs. Part III opens with a consideration of the problems of local work in school and college. Then teachers describe a variety of studies involving local history which they have undertaken with their students and pupils. Finally, there are lists of various types of books which are useful in work of this kind.

Some may claim that what is really needed is a handbook for local studies rather than one which is devoted simply to local history. Certainly from both the academic and the educational point of view it is not always easy, or desirable, to isolate historical aspects or factors from a total environment. But a comprehensive book on local studies would be a long one. It would also repeat much of what is in print since the geographical, ecological and rural studies approaches are already catered for. The approach where the teacher is least well-served is the historical, and it is this want which, it is hoped, may now be supplied. Material more commonly associated with other subjects is discussed where it is fundamental to local history, but more information can be found in specialist books such as C. A. Simpson, *The Study of Local Geography: a Handbook for Teachers* (2nd ed., Methuen, 1950); K. S. Wheeler and M. Harding eds., *Geographical Fieldwork. A Handbook* (Blond Educational, 1965); D. P. Bennett and D. A. Humphries, *Introduction to Field Biology* (Ed. Arnold, 1965); G. D. Fisher, *The Teacher's Book of Nature Study* (Chambers, 1958); and S. McB. Carson and R. W. Colton, *The Teaching of Rural Studies* (Ed. Arnold, 1962).

The debt which the author of a book such as this owes to others is obvious and immense, and I should like to thank all whose work, writings or opinions I have drawn upon. I am especially grateful to the teachers who sent me descriptions of work carried out under their direction: unfortunately, shortage of space has prevented the inclusion of all the examples which were submitted. Some parts of the chapter, 'Geological and Geographical Factors', were first published in *The Amateur Historian*.

R. DOUCH

October, 1966

Part I

The Development and Value of Local History Studies in English Schools

THE EMERGENCE OF THREE TECHNIQUES

Many of even the most ardent supporters of the teaching of local history would probably be surprised to learn that its inclusion in the work of English schools has been persistently advocated since the beginning of the twentieth century. The reasons given for teaching it and the place suggested for it, however, have varied over the years with changing views on both the content of history and the theory of education.

Three major approaches to the use of local history in school have developed.[1] At first, the value of local history was said to lie in the vivid illustrations which it could provide to enliven the generalisations of national history. This view was recommended to teachers in elementary and secondary schools and training colleges in important official publications which followed the 1902 Education Act, and the contribution of local history as 'a fortifying and illustrative auxiliary' has been repeatedly acknowledged ever since.[2] Such illustrations might be of the 'great men, great events' variety, or they could consist of commonplace articles and features, such as tools, costumes, buildings and institutions.

Surprisingly, in view of the importance which had long been attached to community study in, for example, Germany and the United States, it was only in the 'twenties that many English writers and teachers began to consider that local history was worth studying and teaching in its own right or as a starting point from which to work outwards. Pioneers of

[1]A more detailed account of the history of local history in English schools is to be published separately.

[2]See Board of Education, *Handbook of Suggestions for the Consideration of Teachers and Others concerned in the Work of Public Elementary Schools* (H.M.S.O., 1905), p. 63; Board of Education, *Teaching of History in Secondary Schools* (H.M.S.O., 1908), p. 5; and W. M. Childs, *The Teaching of Local History* (Historical Association, Leaflet no. 11, 1908), p. 2. For subsequent publications on the teaching of history, see University of Southampton Institute of Education, *The Teaching of Geography and History and Related Local Studies* (2nd ed., 1957).

the emerging junior school emphasised the vital rôles that activity and the exploration of their immediate environment must play in the education of young children and, contemporaneously, older children began to be involved in local surveys.[1] In its extreme form a survey entailed a scientific study of the locality from every point of view, history having its contribution to make along with geology, geography, botany, folk-lore, economics and planning. But in the hands of a teacher who was especially interested in history, the survey method often came to be employed in considering only, or mainly, local history. A renewed interest in the 'thirties in education for citizenship provided further impetus for the survey approach.[2]

Since 1945 local history has become immensely popular as an adult study. The subject has acquired a new academic standing well exemplified in the establishment and work of the Department of English Local History in the University of Leicester. New sources have also been pressed into service. Archaeological remains, for example, have been recognised as valuable in the study of medieval and modern history and, of even greater significance, the original documents of local history have become available for study on a hitherto unprecedented scale with the widespread establishment of county and county borough record offices. It is not surprising that the work of schools and colleges has been influenced by these developments and it is no exaggeration to say that, since 1945, the study and teaching of local history have become very fashionable. This trend has been further encouraged by the increasing emphasis which educationists have laid on the importance of interpreting the environment to the boys and girls who are growing up in it.[3] Consequently, books and articles published since the war constantly refer to the value of local

[1]See, for example, Board of Education, *Report of the Consultative Committee on the Primary School* (H.M.S.O., 1931) and Board of Education, *Village Survey-Making: an Oxfordshire Experiment* (H.M.S.O., 1929).

[2]See Association for Education in Citizenship, *Education for Citizenship in Elementary Schools* (Oxford University Press, 1939), pp. 155-64.

[3]Ministry of Education, Central Advisory Council for Education (England), *School and Life* (H.M.S.O., 1947), pp. 35-47.

history.[1] Few, however, discuss at any length the best ways of using local material, and the two broad approaches which were distinguished and used before 1939 have continued to be recommended and employed with little comment.

Although it has not often been isolated in descriptions of techniques, a third approach to the use of local material has become increasingly common in practice.[2] This is the method of studying, in detail and in a more scientific manner, an aspect, or aspects, of local history. Sometimes such work resembles the local illustration of a national theme, but more time is devoted to the local material than to the national and instead of the illustration being summarily treated after the discussion of national developments, the wider implications arise out of the local study; at other times, local topics are investigated for their own sake.

Two stages at which local work has become very evident since the war are the junior school and the college of education. While interesting developments in, for instance, the use of the environment and the encouragement of individual studies, were appearing at both levels before 1939, the number and variety of such activities have vastly increased since 1945. Some of these changes have been introduced as History, some as Environmental Studies.

The shortlived post-war social studies movement in non-selective secondary schools continued and developed the immediate pre-war interest in the local survey, and the most recent Ministry publication on environmental work underwrites this approach.[3] Nevertheless, although examples of

[1]See, for example, Ministry of Education, *Teaching History* (H.M.S.O., 1952); D. W. Humphreys, *Local History in School* (National Council of Social Service, 1953); E. M. Lewis, *Teaching History in Secondary Schools* (Evans, 1960); W. H. Burston and C. W. Green eds., *Handbook for History Teachers* (Methuen, 1962); and I.A.A.M., *The Teaching of History in Secondary Schools* (3rd ed., Cambridge University Press, 1965).

[2]But see M. S. Dilke ed., *Field Studies for Schools: I The Purpose and Organisation of Field Studies* (Rivingtons, 1965), p. 45.

[3]See Ministry of Education, *Local Studies* (H.M.S.O., 1948), a Visual Unit including films, film-strips, charts and a booklet. See also E. Layton and J. B. White, *The School Looks Around* (Longmans, 1948).

broadly based local studies are not difficult to find in post-war secondary schools, it is true to say that much of their increased work in local history has taken place within a fairly traditional history syllabus. This pattern has been encouraged by the continuing hold of external examinations on the work of grammar schools and by their introduction into other secondary schools from the early 'fifties. Some examining bodies, however, began actively to promote the study of local history in non-selective schools from the mid-'fifties onwards and when the Certificate of Secondary Education was launched in 1964, provision for work in local history was a most marked feature of the regulations of the new regional boards.

Three broad approaches to local history in school and college have thus emerged—the illustration of national history by local examples, the local survey, and the study of particular aspects of the local community. All are valuable, but it has been unfortunate that the comprehensive and concentrated local survey received so much attention between the mid-'twenties and the early 'fifties. While no local work is easy, this method is often the most difficult to organise successfully and the least certain in its educational achievements. It involves teacher, students and outside people in a vast amount of work; it can be undertaken only occasionally; and it frequently treats many topics in a very superficial manner. Many teachers have been disappointed with the results of their efforts in this field and, as suggested later, more limited investigations are likely to be more rewarding, especially for the beginner.

THE VALUE AND PROBLEMS OF LOCAL HISTORY IN SCHOOL

The benefits to be derived from a study of local history and the problems involved in such work will vary with the content and organisation of specific studies and the age and ability of the participating students. In particular, a great deal depends on how much, and what sort of, work the pupils themselves undertake. Descriptions of, and comments on, some specific projects are included in Part III: here an attempt is made to summarise in general terms the contribution which local history can make to children's education. Much of what is said applies equally well to the work of older students, including teachers and intending teachers.

The benefits which children may obtain from local history studies can be broadly described as educational, psychological and historical. The first two kinds of benefit are associated with most types of environmental work; the third is the especial concern of local history. The general educational value of environmental studies derives from the nature of the content of such studies and is further enhanced by the methods of work which can be employed. There is a reality and obvious significance about local history which is noticeably absent from much of the material contained in conventional syllabuses. Opportunities abound to study real people and situations in depth and detail in contrast with the generalisations and superficial skimming of broad topics which so often occurs. Barriers of all kinds can be broken down. Those between subjects are quickly crossed, local history rarely remaining academic history for long as it links with, for example, geography, art, literature and economics. Closer contacts with parents also often develop as they become involved in such work, as suppliers of information perhaps, or as providers of transport. Most important of all, local history often helps to break down barriers between school and the world. This may be achieved simply through the pupils' realisation of the significance and interest of appropriate and meaningful local material, or it may arise from the direct study of matters of civic importance or social responsibility. It may involve the wider appreciation of the interdependence of members of a community or an introduction to career opportunities for the individual. Or it may be concerned with aesthetic considerations, an awareness of beauty and an interest in the activities of organisations such as archaeological and historical societies and the Civic Trust. Often an enthusiasm may be aroused which will last a lifetime.

The nature of local material, the fact that it is on the doorstep, means that children studying it have many opportunities for active participation in their work. Too much school history teaching consists of the delivery of ready packaged goods. Children need to work on their own more. In local studies they have the advantage, and attraction, of direct experience, and their initiative and attitude of enquiry and discovery can be developed. They can be encouraged to be curious, to observe patiently and accurately, to concentrate, to ask questions, to collect, to classify, and, where appropriate, to see relationships. This spirit of enquiry promotes a healthier attitude to learning and results in the acquisition of more real, as opposed to merely verbal, knowledge, and often leads to the development of more logical thought. Work on the neighbourhood also lends itself to various methods of class organisation, such as individual and group, as well as class, work, and frequently promotes less formal relationships with children. It enables basic skills to be purposefully used in the discovery of new knowledge, and furnishes innumerable occasions for creative activity and the presentation of information in a variety of ways. Furthermore, it provides tasks which offer a sense of adventure and the chance of success to a wide range of individual ability.

Several of the advantages of local work which have been described as educational might also be classified as psychological. There is the additional psychological advantage that local work helps the student to know and to understand the environment and the community of which he forms part. It is often said that local studies are valuable because they utilise the surroundings which a pupil knows: it is truer to say that they first help him to see this environment and then to use it. Such experience is likely to help his development both as an individual and as a member of the community by providing some roots and a sense of belonging as well as a feeling of responsibility.

The more specific advantages of local history as history again overlap with the educational and psychological advantages, especially if a broad view is taken of the nature and purpose of teaching history. History lessons ought to be interesting, but too often they are dull. Frequently one of the reasons for this dullness is remoteness, the content of the lessons having no contact, emotional or material, with the children's lives and experience. One of the great attractions of local history is that it happened here. Because of this it does not follow that it will interest every pupil, but at least there is a link which can be utilised. Furthermore, tangible remains of this local history often survive—a burial mound, a document, a town wall, a tradesman's token, a dress—and it is this which underlines the reality, arouses imaginative sympathy, and facilitates comprehension. Appreciating that the local past is real may help pupils to feel the same towards the general past: it will certainly encourage the development of a more meaningful historical vocabulary as terms are used to describe real objects. In favoured areas where, for example, a wide variety of architectural periods is represented, local remains may help in developing a time sense. Much more important, however, it is impossible to ignore the present in local history studies. Even where local illustrations of national themes are employed, some aspect of that illustration is likely to form part of the contemporary scene: much more obviously, where the local community is surveyed, generally or in parts, the present situation inevitably receives considerable attention. Surely this is important. Too much school history bears no relationship to the world in which pupils will live. Instead of a vague sense of time, should we not be trying to encourage the growth of an awareness of change and a sense of development, an appreciation of the links between past, present and future?

Perhaps one of the most valuable attributes of local history as history is that it provides examples and experiences, at many different levels, of historical method. It is not the only field where source materials are available for children to study, but it is undoubtedly the one where they are often most accessible. Moreover, the lower the age and ability of the children involved, the more likely it is that material suitable for this purpose will need to be taken from the locality. This is not to say that all the sources of local history are easy to handle: they certainly are not. But in their vast range there will be a variety of opportunities for children to take part in the finding-out process, to appreciate the limitations of so-called evidence, and to see how history comes to be written.

The study of local history has its problems as well as its

advantages. Some areas offer fewer possibilities than others. Most schools in the middle of new housing estates are obviously poorly placed compared with those in the heart of York or Winchester. In some areas it may even be almost a first priority to lift children's eyes beyond the immediate environment.[1] Even so, it is surprising how much of interest and value the most unpromising surroundings often yield. There are dangers, too, of over-emphasis and parochialism, of repetition at different stages of school life, and of making it appear that local history is somehow unconnected with national affairs. But these criticisms refer to unsatisfactory methods of using local material rather than to the nature of the material itself.

There are, however, two major groups of problems which any teacher attempting work in local history will quickly encounter. These are fundamental, and neither has received the attention it deserves in most of what has been written on local history in school. On the contrary, local history has usually been assumed to be an easy pursuit, a voyage of discovery on which teacher and taught embark together, innocent and in ignorance. The first group of problems arises out of the number and variety of the source materials with which both teacher and children may need to be familiar. Any student of local history soon discovers that he may be called upon to use written sources, both printed and unprinted, which are unfamiliar to him and which may present many difficulties. Furthermore, he will also have to grapple with other types of sources, such as maps, place names, and architecture, which he has not previously encountered. There are few local aids to guide him to the existing material, and much that he would like to use he discovers, only by bitter experience, is non-existent, inaccessible, or incomprehensible. All his local knowledge will be hard-won and is likely to be dependent upon his remaining in the neighbourhood for some years. The second group of problems consists of those connected with introducing this local material into the work of particular kinds of schools and colleges. Here, again, little guidance has

[1]See e.g. J. B. Mays, *Education and the Urban Child* (Liverpool University Press, 1962), p. 91.

been given. What can be done? How is local history to be fitted into the syllabus? How can particular pieces of work be organised? These are the kinds of practical questions which need to be answered.

It is hoped that Parts II and III will help teachers to deal with these two major problems.

Part II

Sources of Local History

Chapter 1 Introduction

The number and variety of the sources which may have to be consulted in searching for information constitute a major problem in work on many aspects of local history. Until recently few courses were organised to help students and teachers to deal with this problem, and today many, even of those who undergo some academic training in history, still find themselves ill-equipped for work in this field.

Historical source material may be classified in various ways. A broad distinction can be drawn, for example, between written evidence and archaeological remains. Another common method is to distinguish between primary and secondary authorities. It is not always easy to decide in which of these categories some items should be placed, but the former description normally implies that the material so labelled is an original source, for instance, an unpublished document. By contrast, a secondary authority has been edited, integrated or arranged in some way; a popular county history is a good example. Sources may also be differentiated on the basis of their location. Many are to be found in the neighbourhood to which they refer, but a surprisingly large number often lies far away, in the county or diocesan town perhaps, or in a national library or museum, or even overseas.

While all these divisions will be recognisable in the following chapters, the sources are there classified on, what may be termed, a working basis, in the several broad groups in which they will usually be encountered. These are described as books, maps, geological and geographical factors, place names, archaeological remains, buildings, archives, pictorial records, and people. For each type of source its nature is defined, its content considered, its difficulties discussed, and its availability described.

Such sources will be differently used by students and teachers with different objectives. The ambitious local historian who is investigating the history of his community in a comprehensive way must know about and consult all of them. Others may not wish, or need, to make constant or detailed use of every type of material. Thus someone interested in prehistoric life on the chalk downs will consult different kinds of sources from the person who is studying poor law history in his parish. However, a broad familiarity on any teacher's part with all types of sources and some idea of the questions which each may or may not be able to answer will be very useful in helping him to make the most of the opportunities offered by his environment for teaching purposes.

The order of consulting different sources will also vary. There is no set routine, though experience soon teaches several useful general lessons. Thus in many investigations it is wise to study the map before embarking on field work, and it is nearly always advantageous, where both types of sources are relevant, to alternate periods of studying written records with work in the field. There are some kinds of books which repay early consultation in many studies. At the same time, from a teaching point of view, answers are too often provided in secondary authorities before the primary field evidence has been examined. Indeed, in local history studies generally, insufficient attention is paid to field remains. More advice than this it is difficult to give: the student must use his common sense and be always on the look-out for opportunities of integrating sources significantly and for labour-saving short cuts.

A systematic method of note-making and keeping is essential. Different individuals prefer different methods, but some sort of loose-leaf or card-index system is probably best. This enables information to be filed, sorted and cross-referenced easily. Records made in the field or library should be accurate and full enough to be subsequently understood. They should be incorporated into the permanent note system as soon as possible and be given adequate references. It is useless trying to rely on memory. Accordingly, it is also a good idea in many studies always to carry a notebook and a map. In all field work it is important to respect other people's property, to seek permission before venturing on to private land, and to follow the Country Code.

As seen in Part I, the precise nature of the relationship of any local work to national history will vary. Even so, local developments should never be considered without reference to the general background of events. If they are, such studies may lose their perspective, typical customs or occurrences may be considered unique, or, less usually, the real significance of an uncommon feature may be overlooked.

Chapter 2 Books

Books are an obvious and long-established aid to historical enquiry and it is to them that many people interested in local history are likely to turn first for information. There is usually an assortment of published material on most topics. Many indispensable specialised works are recommended in subsequent chapters in connection with particular sources. Here more general works are mentioned, those which, since they cover a variety of subjects, it would be profitable to consult at an early stage in all but the most limited of investigations.

GENERAL WORKS

Several publications have appeared in recent years which deal generally with the content and techniques of local history. Three of these may be recommended as essential reading for anyone who intends working on the history of a locality. W. G. Hoskins, *Local History in England* (Longmans, 1959), describes written and field evidence, and is both informative and inspiring. R. B. Pugh, *How to Write a Parish History* (6th ed. Allen and Unwin, 1954), discusses a multitude of written sources. Finally, there is a journal, *The Amateur Historian* (1952-), now published quarterly by the National Council of Social Service; some of its articles are referred to later, but there are many others which are valuable, especially those on a variety of field and written sources. Several organisations publish general pamphlets which are of interest to the local historian: the most useful are the Historical Association, 59A, Kennington Park Road, London, S.E.11, and the National Council of Social Service, 26, Bedford Square, London, W.C.1. D. W. Humphreys and F. G. Emmison, *Local History for Students* (1966) is an introductory pamphlet published by the latter.

In connection with work on a local topic, it will usually be necessary to consult relevant background books. It is essential that such general works should be accurate and authoritative. There are so many incorrect or out of date books available that it is all too easy to read the wrong ones. To avoid doing this the general books recommended in later chapters should be supplemented by reference to recently published bibliographies. Two, in particular, are invaluable. F. W. Kuhlicke and F. G. Emmison eds., *English Local History Handlist* (3rd ed., Historical Association, 1965) provides the untrained investigator with a series of short book-lists on most of the topics which he is likely to encounter in his local history studies. Almshouses, boroughs, cock-fighting, documentary sources, and earthworks are random selections from the early part of its index and give a good idea of its broad coverage. The Council for British Archaeology, *British Archaeology: a Book-list* (The Council, 1960) does the same for archaeological topics. Since archaeology is there interpreted as the study of the material remains of the past up to 1750, this list includes not only a wealth of references to prehistoric and early historic Britain, but also the titles of books dealing with topics such as settlement, architecture, costume and crafts to the middle of the eighteenth century. R. Douch, *A Handbook of Local History: Dorset, with a Supplement of Additions and Corrections to 1960* (University of Bristol, 1962) contains much information on books and other sources which is useful to students in other counties.

LOCAL BIBLIOGRAPHIES AND HISTORIES

In seeking printed material which will supply information about a particular neighbourhood, it is very easy to waste time in a desultory and undirected search. It is wise, therefore, to plan one's reading, though not too rigidly. There are certain kinds of books which can be consulted with great profit in the early stages of many specialised, as well as general, enquiries. If these are referred to in the suggested sequence much time can be saved by acquiring, in the most convenient form, information which is included in a variety of publications. Moreover, such a plan frequently helps to set the general scene or to lay down the outlines for the study of a subject. It also reveals what work has already been done, thus perhaps avoiding repeating it unnecessarily.

One of the first kinds of books to be sought should again be bibliographies, this time lists of books relating to the neighbourhood. Essex and Oxfordshire are amongst the counties which have comprehensive printed bibliographies, while work is in progress on such lists in, for example, Hertfordshire and Lancashire. But it is a sad commentary on the present state of English local history studies that so few counties and towns have good modern bibliographies from which a student can quickly discover the work that has already been done on the locality. If there is no detailed survey, other more limited, but still useful, bibliographical aids may have been compiled. A general guide has perhaps been issued. A good example of such a publication is A. G. Dickens and K. A. MacMahon, *A Guide to Regional Studies on the East Riding of Yorkshire and the City of Hull* (University of Hull, 1956): there are others, for Surrey and Leicestershire, for example. Sometimes a local periodical publication will contain lists of relevant works. J. P. Anderson, *The Book of British Topography* (London, Satchell, 1881) and A. L. Humphreys, *A Handbook of County Bibliography* (London, The Author, 1917), although old books, are still worth consulting for many localities. P. Stockham and J. Rogers, *British Local History: a Selected Bibliography* (Dillon's University Bookshop, 1964), a guide to books in print at the time of publication, has useful county and general sections. Public libraries often have printed or typescript lists of local works or catalogues of their own collections, such as *Books and Maps relating to Huntingdonshire in the County Library* and *Basic Books on Sheffield History*. By their very nature book-lists rapidly become out of date. There is no easy way of remedying this defect, but searching the card indexes of local library stock is a valuable method of gathering references, and quick consultation of *The British Humanities Index: County Lists* (Library Association, 1962-, formerly *Subject Index to Periodicals*) and the Council for British Archaeology's *Archaeological Bibliography for Great Britain and*

Ireland (annual, 1950-) will supply details of any recent work.

The county has been a popular unit in the study of English local history ever since the pioneer work of Leland, Camden, Speed and their fellow antiquarians in the sixteenth and early seventeenth centuries. Consequently, county histories of various kinds line the library shelves and constitute the next books to seek out. The first county history which should be consulted is the *Victoria County History*. The *V.C.H.* was conceived in the late nineteenth century when a scheme was devised for the publication of a new large-scale county history, based on original research, for every county in England, except Northumberland for which a history on similar lines had been started a few years previously. County volumes were to be financed by the local gentry, and the project began in promising fashion. But the early rate of publication was not maintained as administrative and financial problems arose. The University of London became responsible for the series in the early 'thirties and, with changing social conditions, new sources of income—local industries and local authorities, for example—have been tapped, especially since 1945. By 1966 one hundred and thirty-eight volumes had appeared, but for only a dozen counties was the history complete.

The broad arrangement of the volumes is the same for all counties. Volumes I and II usually deal with general aspects of county history, such as the archaeological remains of different periods, political developments, and social and economic changes. Subsequent volumes, the number depending on the size of the county being described, contain accounts of the individual parishes within it. These are classified under hundreds and wards, the old sub-divisions of the shire, and the easiest way to locate references to a specific place is by using the general index. The parts of the *V.C.H.* that have been published for individual counties vary considerably so that the student cannot be certain what he will find when he starts work in any area. Thus eight volumes cover Lancashire; six out of nine Sussex volumes have appeared, and work is still in progress; for Dorset only one volume, volume II, which, according to the general plan of the series, deals mainly with ecclesiastical history, has been published. The date of publication of the local *V.C.H.* is an important consideration. Many are now forty or fifty years old and represent an approach to local history which was affected by its links with the local nobility and gentry and which is now, in some respects, outdated. Indeed, some critics maintain that even recently published volumes are too traditional in their approach and content. The practical outcome of this for the investigator is that he will find very detailed entries about the families and estates of large landholders, ecclesiastical architecture, the right to present the parson to the living, and charities, but very little information on those aspects of the social and economic life of the community generally in which historians have become interested in recent decades. But, whatever its limitations, the *V.C.H.* still stands as the first of the county histories to be consulted.

Search should next be made for any county histories written between the late sixteenth and the late nineteenth centuries. These were usually the work of squires or professional men, such as parsons, lawyers or doctors, and they often run into several large volumes. William Lambarde's *The Perambulation of Kent*, published in 1576, and Richard Carew's *Survey of Cornwall* which followed in 1602 were the first of a long line. Between 1600 and 1800 some fifty of these large-scale histories appeared and there is scarcely a county which cannot boast at least one example of such a work. They have their limitations, of course. Thus, even more than the *V.C.H.* their content is restricted by their patronage; some writers are more reliable than others; and prehistoric and archaeological information is often suspect. But again, whatever detrimental may be said about these county histories, works of this type, such as Hutchins' *Dorset*, Hasted's *Kent*, or Dugdale's *Warwickshire*, remain not only as monuments to massive labours undertaken in circumstances which lacked so many of the modern aids to study, but also as indispensable sources of information.

Since the late nineteenth century many short single-volume county histories have been written. These are often more in the nature of guide-books, which are considered later, and their information is rarely based on original material. Some represent individual publishing ventures of which nothing can be said here, except that some are better than others. Often, however, they form part of a publisher's series. Few of these succeed in covering every county. The volumes in *The Making of the English Landscape* series (Hodder and Stoughton) provide a very useful introduction to a locality and it is unfortunate that only some half-a-dozen counties have been treated in it. The *Oxford County Histories for Schools,* about fifteen volumes of which were published between 1908 and 1915, are old, but not always outdated. The illustrations in the wide-ranging and much-used *Queen's* (*King's*) *England* series (Hodder and Stoughton) are much better than the text which is flowery and sometimes unreliable. Darwen Finlayson's *County Histories* have only a brief text, but contain useful maps and illustrations. There are three other series which may be singled out for particular mention. These are available for most counties and although the quality of individual volumes again varies, these series as a whole have been found to be valuable and reliable. Two are now out of print, the *Highways and Byways in . . .* series (Macmillan) which, although arranged in guide-book tours, includes a great deal of historical information, and the so-called *Cambridge County Geographies* which embrace archaeology and history as well as geography. The third, a newer venture, is the *County Books* series, together with its near relation, *Regional Books,* both published by Hale.

After county histories, relevant town histories and/or village histories should be identified and examined. While John Stow's *Survey of London* appeared as early as 1598 most existing town histories were written in the eighteenth and nineteenth centuries. They are usually repositories of archaeological, constitutional and ecclesiastical material rather than real histories, and supply information on these, and other, subjects which varies in amount and reliability with the author's interests and qualifications. Thus Southampton is much better served by its late nineteenth century history, written by a local parson, than is Portsmouth, where the twentieth century account is the work of a busy newspaperman. Given the limitations indicated above, the old *Historic Towns* series (Longmans) and the Batsford *Cities and Towns* series are useful. A few admirable urban histories have appeared recently, such as those for Bury St. Edmunds, Lincoln and Newcastle, and the volumes published by the British Association describing the places where its annual conference is held are invaluable. But many towns are still without a good history.

Histories of parishes began to be written in the seventeenth century. The trickle continued in the eighteenth century and became a flood in the nineteenth. Printing costs were low and country parsons, in particular, often wrote a parish history. It is surprising how frequently a so-called history of the parish in which one is interested has been published. But again the approach is usually from the standpoint of the upper classes and the contents are often assembled uncritically. The quality of such works is very variable and the reliability of individual volumes should always be checked before their statements are accepted. In recent years a large number of interesting scrapbooks has been compiled by groups such as Women's Institutes and Community Councils. These are often well worth tracking down: only a few have been published.

Besides these general histories of counties, towns and parishes, books will be found dealing with particular topics in relation to each unit. Many of these are written on a county basis. Thus much primary source material is available covering many topics from late Saxon charters to twentieth century Development Plans. Secondary sources arranged in this way—*Field Archaeology as illustrated by Hampshire* and *Legends and Traditions of Huntingdonshire*, for example—are commoner still. Such books will be comparatively rare for parishes, but it is, of course, likely that there will be more of them for towns. If the local county, city or borough council, library, museum or historical societies are enterprising, they will probably have published a variety of useful booklets. Libraries and museums may also have collections of pamphlets, cuttings, and other ephemeral material.

In many areas literary associations give rise to another valuable group of books. Some of these may result simply from the fact that a famous author was born, or lived, in the neighbourhood. Others may provide some of the essential material of local history itself, as in the books by and about authors like Gilbert White or Thomas Hardy. See J. Freeman, *Literature and Locality* (Cassell, 1963).

PERIODICAL PUBLICATIONS

A great deal of material on specialised aspects of local history is in the form, not of books, but of articles. Many students feel that such papers in learned periodicals are bound to be too advanced for them. Often this is not true, in fact, because in an article a considerable amount of space is usually devoted to the description or elucidation of a restricted theme. Relevant articles may appear in many different national journals. The most important specialised periodicals are mentioned in later chapters. There are also more general publications. Some of these, *Notes and Queries* and *The Gentleman's Magazine* for instance, are well-indexed. But many journals are not. Fortunately there are several aids to using them, especially Sir G. L. Gomme's *Index of Archaeological Papers, 1665-1890* with annual *Supplements* to 1909 (Constable, 1892-1914); E. L. C. Mullins, *Guide to Historical and Archaeological Publications of English and Welsh Societies, 1901-33* (forthcoming); and A. T. Milne comp., *Writings on British History* (Royal Historical Society, 1937-).

There are certain local periodicals which may include papers on almost any topic of local interest: these must be searched in detail. The most important will probably be the annual *Papers and Proceedings* of the county society, the members of which are likely to be interested in geology, natural history and archaeology as well as in local history. Every county has at least one of these societies, usually called a field, archaeological, architectural, antiquarian or natural science club or society. Details of such societies can be found in S. E. Harcup, *Historical, Archaeological and Kindred Societies in the British Isles* (Institute of Historical Research, 1965). These bodies hold meetings and organise excursions: they often maintain a museum or a library. Membership is open to all and although some are still unduly influenced by their upper and upper-middle class origin, anyone seriously interested in local history should certainly join his county society. Besides enjoying any facilities that the society offers, he will also have the opportunity of meeting people with interests similar to his own. Since many county societies have been in existence for a century or more, they now boast about a hundred volumes of *Proceedings*. Unfortunately these are not always adequately indexed. Similar societies, some of them publishing societies, exist for many towns and districts. Other relevant local periodicals, many of them published once again on a county basis, range from learned, through semi-popular, to popular publications: *Notes and Queries*, available for many counties; *The Cheshire Historian*; *Northamptonshire, Past and Present*; and *Hampshire, The County Magazine*, illustrate this variety. Some of these journals are still issued: some are now defunct.

VISITORS' DESCRIPTIONS, GUIDE BOOKS, DIRECTORIES AND NEWSPAPERS

Most of the printed material so far described would be classified as secondary in nature. There are four additional categories which are often worth consulting at an early stage: with these, more of the material is of a primary character. The first category consists of descriptions of the locality written by visitors. Natives or residents may have left diaries or descriptions concerning the neighbourhood: if they have, and if this material has been published, it is likely to be listed in local bibliographies. The visitors' descriptions, which are especially valuable from the late sixteenth to the early nineteenth century, are more easily overlooked. Some of the authors of such accounts may be famous; for example, John Leland, Samuel Pepys, Daniel Defoe or J. B. Priestley: others may be comparatively or completely unknown. Some descriptions may be unpublished, but it is surprising how many accounts are readily available in print for many localities. An indication of the amount and variety of material relating to a single town which can be derived from this source, as well as a list of generally useful descriptions, is provided by the author's *Southampton, c.1540-1956: Visitors' Descriptions* (Southampton Corporation, 1961).

From the eighteenth century onwards more and more people journeyed throughout England for pleasure. Guide-books developed to meet their needs. Much of the information contained in some recent volumes, as well as in many early ones, is unreliable and, in general, a broad distinction can be drawn between the historical and the contemporary material which they contain. The former often needs to be used with care and can usually be checked elsewhere. The latter is normally most detailed in guide-books published between the late eighteenth and mid-nineteenth centuries. Before then the accounts tend to be in the nature of general descriptive surveys which frequently cover several counties: afterwards the guide-book is often part of a national series which left much of the detailed local information to be provided by other publications. Most guide-books for this period are especially rich in information relating to local inhabitants, institutions and societies, and building activities, as well as in advertisements. In 1850 John Murray joined A. and C. Black as publishers of local guide-books on a national scale and, by the turn of the century, Murray's *Handbooks for Travellers* were available for every English county. Volumes in this series, like the Ward Lock *Red Guides*, published since the late nineteenth century, can often be bought cheaply secondhand and are well worth acquiring. Two useful current series, neither of which, unfortunately, covers the whole country are the *Little Guides* (Methuen) and the *Shell Guides* (Faber). Locally published guide-books, many of which are officially approved by the local authority, are available today for most areas: unfortunately, the quality of both their production and content often leaves much to be desired.

Directories and gazetteers provide in more detail some of the information which was frequently included in early guide-books. Primarily commercial in origin, they began to appear in the late eighteenth century. They are still published today, though their heyday was perhaps between the 1830's and the 1930's. Their information is not always accurate and, like guide-books, they are sometimes difficult to date. J. C. Norton,

Guide to the National and Provincial Directories of England and Wales, excluding London, published before 1856 (Royal Historical Society, 1950) is a useful reference list. Early volumes were usually published locally, then, as with guide-books, national publishers also entered the field, so that the directories of, for example, Pigot and Co., the Post Office, William White and Kelly, were produced for many counties and towns. Most early directories consisted mainly of lists of the chief inhabitants and their occupations. Later, details of shops, markets, services and transport, together with a general historical and contemporary description of the locality were added, until by the middle of the nineteenth century the directory looked very much like its twentieth century successor. More specialised directories, such as *Trades' Directories* and *Diocesan Directories,* are also valuable. National gazetteers may be worth consulting: two useful ones are N. Carlisle, *A Topographical Dictionary of England,* 2 vols. (Longman and Co., 1808) and S. Lewis, *A Topographical Dictionary of England,* 4 vols. (7th ed., London, 1849).

Finally there are newspapers. The national press may contain material for the local historian, but normally local newspapers will provide him with much more. The origin of the modern newspaper goes back to the Civil War period in the seventeenth century. But the first national daily was not established until 1702 and, although many local papers appeared in the eighteenth century, it was only in the nineteenth that they began to report local affairs in great detail instead of concentrating mainly on national news. For approximately the last one hundred and fifty years, therefore, local papers are an invaluable source on topics such as the physical growth of the neighbourhood, local politics and government, parliamentary history, social and economic life and the work of the courts. Many small papers are now defunct or have been absorbed into larger concerns. The standard of reporting varies and political bias is often discernible. Searching newspapers often takes a long time since they are seldom indexed and there is invariably so much that is interesting, but irrelevant, to scan. The Times, *Tercentenary Handlist of English and Welsh Newspapers, 1620-1920* (London, 1920) and Mitchell's *Newspaper Press Directory* (annual, 1846-, published by Benn since 1948) will help in identifying newspapers covering a specific neighbourhood. See also D. Read, 'North of England Newspapers (*c.*1700-*c.*1900) and their Value to Historians' in *Proceedings of the Leeds Philosophical Society*, vol. viii (1957). News sheets in parish magazines are a related source which should not be overlooked.

ADDRESSES

THE LOCAL PUBLIC LIBRARY. Most public libraries have a 'Local Collection' of material relating to the neighbourhood. Some books may be available on loan, but a great many will, because of their rarity, be for reference only. The scope of these collections, the area which they cover, and the facilities provided in the way of accommodation, classification and catalogues vary enormously, so that it is impossible to predict what may be found in any particular place. Generally speaking, collections in borough libraries are perhaps more comprehensive and better organised than those in county libraries because they were established earlier. However, with the increasing interest shown in local history since 1945, both types of library have expanded and developed their local collections, and still further improvement can be expected. Whatever the facilities which a specific library is able to offer, the serious student can be sure of a warm welcome. See J. L. Hobbs, *Local History and the Library* (Deutsch, 1962).

Books which are not in stock can usually be borrowed through the Inter-Library Lending Service: details of this service will be supplied by the librarian.

LOCAL SOCIETY LIBRARIES. Many county archaeological and historical societies have valuable collections of local books and other materials. Occasionally, as with the library of the Bristol and Gloucestershire Archaeological Society which has been deposited in the Gloucester City Library, such collections will be found in the public library. More usually they are housed, often with a museum, in the headquarters of the society: Dorset, Surrey and Sussex, for example, have such libraries at Dorchester, Guildford and Lewes respectively. They exist principally for the use of members, but readers are often admitted for a nominal fee.

There are other private libraries not associated with a county society which have local collections: the John Rylands Library, Manchester, is an outstanding example.

LOCAL BOOKSELLERS. Some books on local history can be bought secondhand quite cheaply, but many are expensive. It is always worth looking for books away from the locality with which they are concerned: the price is likely to be lower.

LOCAL NEWSPAPER OFFICES. Back files are often kept and may be consulted. They are usually incomplete, but can often be supplemented from newspaper collections in local and national libraries.

UNIVERSITY LIBRARIES. Most universities have special collections relating to their neighbourhood to which non-members of the university may be admitted. University Extra-Mural Department and Institute of Education Libraries may also contain some relevant material. Some universities have exceptional local history collections with national, rather than regional, coverage: the most important are The University Library, Cambridge; The Institute of Historical Research, University of London; The Bodleian Library, Oxford; and The Borthwick Institute of Historical Research, York.

In addition to the kinds of books mentioned above, unpublished theses may be available: topics which these often cover include geology and geography, and the history of agriculture, industry, commerce and education. *An Index to Theses Accepted for Higher Degrees in the Universities of Great Britain and Ireland*, 1950- (1953-) is published by Aslib, 3, Belgrave Square, London, S.W.1: many earlier ones are listed in the *Theses Supplement*, 1931- (1933-): issued by the University of London Institute of Historical Research.

THE BRITISH MUSEUM LIBRARY, BLOOMSBURY, LONDON, W.C.1. Books which cannot be located elsewhere may often be found in the British Museum. Local libraries should always be searched before application is made for a reader's ticket to the British Museum. The Museum has a large collection of newspapers: the pre-nineteenth century material is housed in the Museum itself and the later papers at Colindale, near Hendon. Details of the British Museum and the use of its facilities are contained in *The British Museum: A Guide to its Public Services* (The Trustees, 1962).

Chapter 3 Maps

Topographical maps represent in two dimensions parts of the earth's surface or selected features on it. Their usefulness, especially in indicating distance and direction, has long been apparent to man, and maps of a sort have been made from the time of the Ancient Egyptians. But it is only during the last four centuries that the technical problems involved in surveying the landscape accurately and in representing the results successfully on a plane have gradually been mastered. Thus, while the student may expect maps to be a useful source in his local history studies, they are likely to be drawn to a small scale and to be inaccurate by modern standards until comparatively recent times.

There are three major groups of maps which are useful in work on local history: for convenience, these may be called modern maps, historical maps, and, rather paradoxically, modern historical maps.

MODERN MAPS

Most of the indispensable modern maps are produced by the Ordnance Survey. These not only supply invaluable information about the general physical setting in which local history has taken place and about particular geographical features, but, because the Survey's officers have always been interested in field antiquities and history, they also include a great deal of purely archaeological and historical information. The Ordnance Survey classifies its maps, some of which are coloured and some black and white, according to scale—small, medium and large—and publishes booklets describing the various maps currently available in each division. Those which are most helpful to the local historian are considered here. It should be noted that the names commonly used to describe maps on some scales (for example, 25 ins. to 1 ml.) do not represent the exact scale to which they are drawn. Further details can be obtained from the booklets and from specimens of the maps themselves.

Two small scale maps provide very general background information for any locality. These are the maps on the scale of 10 mls. to 1 in. (1/625,000) and 4 mls. to 1 in. (1/250,000). With the former, two large sheets cover Great Britain. The two dozen or so subjects of the separate maps include Administrative Areas (counties, county boroughs, urban and rural districts, but not parishes), Solid Geology, Types of Farming, Population and Local Accessibility. The 4 mls. to 1 in. map, familiar especially to motorists as the ¼ in. to 1 ml., is available in regional sheets with titles such as 'England South' and 'The Border'. For a few areas only, such as Greater London and Norwich, there are District Maps on the scale of ½ in. to 1 ml. County diagrams showing local government, parish and parliamentary boundaries are published on the same scale and are often convenient for plotting information on a county basis.

The last, and undoubtedly the most useful, small scale map is the 1 in. to 1 ml. (1/63,360). Often carried in the hiker's knapsack, this is probably the best known of Ordnance Survey publications. It provides a general view of physical and human geography, showing towns and villages, rivers and streams, roads and paths, and contours at fifty-foot intervals, as well as many antiquities. But the scale is still too small for the map to be of much help in the detailed study of a small area. For some half a dozen areas of special interest to holidaymakers, such as the Lake District and the Wye Valley, a Tourist Edition is published. An outline edition, valuable for recording purposes, is also available.

The publications in the large scale group are correctly called plans and not maps. This is because they do not involve distortion, such as there is, for example, in the road widths as shown on the 1 in. map. Two scales are relevant, both of which show great detail. The 50 ins. to 1 ml. (1/1,250), the largest scale published by the Ordnance Survey and confined to urban areas, is available for most large towns and will eventually cover all towns with a population of more than approximately 20,000. For much local work this scale is too large: details obscure the general picture and the large number of sheets required for a small area is costly. The second large scale plan, the 25 ins. to 1 ml. (1/2,500), is much more generally useful. It covers all parts of the country except mountains and moorland wastes. On this map individual streets, houses and gardens, buildings, plots (of which the acreage is given) and boundaries are readily identifiable: a great deal of archaeological and historical information is also included. The last revision of particular sheets may not have taken place very recently and sheets often have to be brought up to date by the purchaser, a useful exercise.

Medium scale maps are described last because there are two scales in this group with which the local historian must be familiar. These are the 2½ ins. to 1 ml. (1/25,000) and the 6 ins. to 1 ml. (1/10,560). The 2½ in., an attractively produced map introduced in 1945, is often the biggest scale on which a parish appears on a single sheet. It gives a fair amount of local detail, including individual buildings, most fences and contours at 25 ft. intervals, in a regional setting, and is very useful for work in the field. It is supplied in outline, coloured and administrative area editions. The 6 ins. to 1 ml. map is the largest scale on which the whole of Great Britain is mapped. All ground features, except some streets in built-up areas, are to scale, and all field boundaries are shown. It is ideal for recording field sites and land-use, and similar studies, as well as being in itself a source of much valuable information.

Three other kinds of modern maps must also be mentioned. Many students will need to consult Geological Maps: these reveal the rocks which underlie the neighbourhood and which, as described in the next chapter, may well have exerted a profound influence on its historical development. ¼ in. and 6 ins. to 1 ml. maps are printed for certain areas, but, for most localities, the most useful published geological map is likely to be the 1 in. to 1 ml. The Geological Survey completed a 1 in. survey of England between 1835 and 1883. The stocks of all ¼ in. and 1 in. sheets were destroyed during the last war: some sheets have been reprinted and a new survey is being made. There are three kinds of geological maps: one shows the 'solid' geology, that is the nature of the underlying rocks, the others 'solid with drift' or 'drift'. The surface deposits, such as alluvium, sands and gravels, which constitute 'drift' are often very significant in the history of a locality and so it is essential that anyone using 1 in. geological maps is familiar with this distinction and aware of the nature of the sheets that he uses.

In Great Britain, rocks and soils are often closely related. The Ordnance Survey has undertaken, as a long-term project, the publication of 1 in. to 1 ml. Soil Maps. Not many have been produced so far, and so the chances of a particular area having been covered are not high.

The last of the modern maps are those of the Land Utilisation Survey. In the early 1930's the whole country was mapped on the 6 ins. to 1 ml. scale and 1 in. to 1 ml. sheets were published showing arable, grass, waste, land used for industrial purposes and so on, together with an accompanying *Report* for each administrative county. In the late 'fifties and early 'sixties a more detailed land utilisation survey was undertaken. Several sheets have already been published on the larger scale of 2½ ins. to 1 ml.

HISTORICAL MAPS

Historical maps may be defined for present purposes as maps made in the past which portray, or attempt to portray, some aspect or aspects of the then contemporary landscape. Few relevant maps survive from the Middle Ages and those which do are of limited value in local work since they usually depict either the whole of the then known world or, at least, most of Britain. The *Mappa Mundi* (*c.*1300) preserved in Hereford Cathedral is a good example of the former, the Matthew Paris map (*c.*1250) and the so-called Gough Map (*c.*1360) of the latter; all are published and are worth consulting for regional detail. Towards the end of the Middle Ages the practice of charting Mediterranean areas for sailors, begun in the twelfth century, was extended to the Atlantic seaboard of Europe with the result that some of the later charts include parts of the coast of Britain. From the late sixteenth century, with the growing mastery of technique and the increasing demand, many more maps were produced and are available. Even so, until the early nineteenth century, they often suffer from the disadvantages of small scale and inaccuracy which have already been mentioned.

County Maps

Many maps of individual counties were published between the late sixteenth and the early nineteenth century. Christopher Saxton (*c*.1542-1611) and John Norden (1548-1625) were the pioneer surveyors and cartographers, the former compiling the first atlas of the English counties. Many later cartographers, notably John Speed and Dutchmen such as Blaeu, used the results of this early work to produce their own maps. Early county maps show little detail: towns and villages are indicated by semi-pictorial symbols, high ground is represented by hillocks, and few roads are marked. Both the quantity and quality of county maps improved from the late seventeenth century onwards, and they are often very useful sources. After John Ogilby's pioneer work in the 1670's, for example, most maps showed roads, and larger scales were often used. Many county maps and their makers are listed in standard reference works. In 1791 the Ordnance Survey was established to provide more systematic map coverage of the whole country, especially for military purposes: consequently the smaller number of private enterprise county maps produced since the early nineteenth century is not such an important source. Nevertheless, some, such as the county political maps made by the brothers C. and J. Greenwood in the 1820's are very useful, not least for their delineation of the boundaries of ecclesiastical parishes before many of them underwent their nineteenth and twentieth century changes.

Maps of Rural Areas

Two types can be distinguished under this heading, the first private, the second more public, in character. The first type includes maps of estates of various kinds, such as manors, houses, farms, parks and mines. A few of these survive from the late Middle Ages, their number increases greatly for the Tudor and Stuart period, and they are plentiful from about 1700 onwards.

Most maps of the second type have been made since the late eighteenth century and are associated with the development of public utilities. Often, before a particular undertaking could proceed, a copy of the proposed development, together with a map, had to be made available for consultation in the locality which would be affected by it. Such maps are frequently drawn to a large scale and often show the suggested scheme and a strip of land on both sides. Services, the provision of which gave rise to large numbers of these maps, include turnpike roads, canals, railways, gas, water, electricity and main drainage.

There are two maps which are especially informative. They exist for many parishes, are large scale, and date from a significant period in the history of the countryside. Between *c.*1760 and 1840 the enclosure of common arable, pasture and waste land by private Act of Parliament, in an effort to increase the food supply, gave rise to a large number of Enclosure Awards and Maps. These define the re-allocation of land and detail the new private owners and the distribution and acreage of their holdings. Occasionally a map was made of the system which was being swept away.

Many parishes did not experience parliamentary enclosure and so have no enclosure map: even with those which did, only a part of the parish, and often a very small part, was affected. Tithe Maps, on the other hand, are much more widely available and usually cover all, or most, of the parish. These were made *c.*1838-54, after the Tithes' Commutation Act of 1836 had converted the rector's right to a tenth part of the produce of the land in his parish into an annual rent charge. Tithe Maps, usually drawn to a scale of between 13 and 26 ins. to 1 ml., and Apportionment Awards delineate the extent of the ecclesiastical parish and show topographical features, roads, paths, names and boundaries, and give the names of all owners and occupiers of titheable land, its acreage, and the use to which it was put. A special printing of the first edition of the 1 in. Ordnance Survey map called the *Index to Tithe Survey* shows the parishes for which a survey was made.

Town Maps

Maps described in the preceding section may also be available for parts of towns. As for maps of the whole of a town, generally speaking the smaller the town was, the less likelihood there is of finding any early map of it. Larger towns often have an increasing number of maps from the late sixteenth century, many of which were made either to show town property or for purposes of defence. Some general town plans are included at the edge of early county maps, and separate town plans were common by the eighteenth century. More and more have been produced since then, amongst which street plans, frequently included in guide-books, are a useful and neglected source.

Early Ordnance Survey Maps

Since the Ordnance Survey has been established for more than a hundred and fifty years, many of its publications are now maps of historical value. There is an indispensable guide to these maps by J. B. Harley. This describes in detail the maps which have been published: over the years many new series and new editions of maps of all scales have been produced, sheet lines have changed, and techniques have altered. The guide is also helpful in dating specific maps which may be discovered.

The earliest Ordnance Survey maps published were on the 1 in. to 1 ml. scale: the whole of England and Wales was covered between 1801 and 1873. The survey for the first 6 in. map began in 1840 and for the 25 in. in 1853: both were completed just before 1900. Many little-known town plans have been produced: the largest, covering some four hundred towns *c.*1870-80 on the scale of approximately 10½ ft. to 1 ml. (1/500) shows minute detail.

Maps

It is usually possible to arrange for reproductions to be made of most kinds of historical maps by one or other of several modern processes. Reproductions have sometimes been published.

HISTORICAL PERIOD MAPS

The Ordnance Survey has published several maps which represent modern attempts to reconstruct past landscapes. All are small scale (15 mls. to 1 in., 1/1,000,000, or 10 mls. to 1 in., 1/625,000) and provide regional rather than very local information. The former are printed on one sheet, the latter on two, one for the north and one for the south of Britain. Each has an accompanying explanatory booklet. The most useful are as follows:

Ancient Britain: 10 mls. to 1 in.: this shows all major archaeological remains above the ground from prehistory to the Norman Conquest.

Southern Britain in the Iron Age: 10 mls. to 1 in.: Britain south of a line from Scarborough to the Isle of Man during the thousand years before the Roman conquest.

Roman Britain: 15 mls. to 1 in.: Roman towns, villas, roads, signal stations, potteries, mines, etc. of the occupation period, A.D. 43-410.

Britain in the Dark Ages: 15 mls. to 1 in.: from the departure of the Romans to the time of Alfred.

Monastic Britain: 10 mls. to 1 in.: this shows all the religious houses of medieval Britain and certain other ecclesiastical information.

Map of England in the Seventeenth Century: 15 mls. to 1 in.: England after the Civil War.

The following maps of special areas have also been published: Celtic Earthworks of Salisbury Plain; Neolithic Maps of Wessex, the Trent Basin, and South Wales; and Hadrian's Wall.

Not all historical period maps are in print. More than one edition of some has been issued: it is always advisable to consult the most recent.

BOOKS

D. Sylvester, *Map and Landscape* (Philip, 1952) is a useful introduction to the study of topographical maps.

General accounts of maps published by the Ordnance Survey are given in *A Description of Ordnance Survey Small Scale Maps* (Ordnance Survey, Chessington, 1957), . . . *Medium Scale Maps* (1955), and . . . *Large Scale Plans* (1954).

Geological maps are considered in K. W. Earle, *The Geological Map* (Methuen, 1936).

The location and nature of various kinds of historical map are discussed in:

G. R. Crone, *Early Maps of the British Isles, A.D. 1000-1579* (Royal Geographical Society, 1961): reproductions, commentary and bibliography.

A. H. W. Robinson, *Marine Cartography in Britain. A History of the Sea Chart to 1855* (Leicester University Press, 1962).

T. Chubb, *The Printed Maps in the Atlases of Great Britain and Ireland: a Bibliography, 1579-1870* (The Homeland Association, 1927) and E. M. Rodger, *The Large Scale County Maps of the British Isles, 1596-1850: A Union List* (Oxford, Bodleian Library, 1960).

Descriptive lists have been published for some individual counties: a good example is P. D. A. Harvey and H. Thorpe, *The Printed Maps of Warwickshire, 1576-1900* (Warwickshire County Council, 1959).

H. G. Fordham, *The Road Books and Itineraries of Great Britain, 1570 to 1850* (Cambridge University Press, 1924).

H. C. Prince, 'The Tithe Surveys of the Mid-Nineteenth Century', *Agricultural History Review*, vol. vii (1959).

J. B. Harley, *The Historian's Guide to Ordnance Survey Maps* (National Council of Social Service, 1964).

F. G. Emmison, *Catalogue of Maps in the Essex Record Office, 1566-1855*, and *Supplements* 1 and 2 (Chelmsford, 1947-1964): a useful survey of the kinds of maps to be found in county record offices.

ADDRESSES

The following addresses should also assist the student in his search for maps of a specific locality.

THE ORDNANCE SURVEY, ROMSEY ROAD, MAYBUSH, SOUTHAMPTON. The Survey publishes *A List of Agents for Ordnance Survey Maps*. These agents, who are to be found in most large towns, stock specimens and index diagrams of maps of all scales. The methods used in numbering sheets and ways of identifying sheets for a particular area are described in the Ordnance Survey booklets, *A Description of . . .*, already mentioned. Maps required for educational purposes should be ordered direct from the Survey itself on Form O.S. 318 since they are then subject to discount. Maps obtainable from the Ordnance Survey include all modern O.S. topographical maps, geological maps, soil maps and historical period maps. For details of publications, latest editions and prices, see Ordnance Survey, *Maps and Plans: general information and price list*. There is also a monthly *Publications Report*.

THE GEOLOGICAL SURVEY AND MUSEUM, EXHIBITION ROAD, SOUTH KENSINGTON, LONDON, S.W.7. *A List of Geological Survey Maps* (The Museum) gives details of all the Survey's published maps. Books and maps, including unpublished 6 ins. to 1 ml. geological maps of some areas, can be studied in the library.

E. STANFORD LTD., 12-14, LONG ACRE, LONDON, W.C.2. This firm sells most kinds of modern maps. These include the limited number of original 1 in. to 1 ml. L.U.S. Maps and *Reports* which are still available and, as they are produced, the sheets of the new 2½ ins. to 1 ml. Land Utilisation Survey. The 6 in. field sheets of the 1930's survey can be seen at the London School of Economics, Houghton Street, Aldwych, London, W.C.2. Unpublished material relating to the more recent survey may be seen, by arrangement with Miss A. Coleman, at King's College, Strand, London, W.C.2.

J. D. POTTER LTD., 145, MINORIES, LONDON, E.C.3. Agent for Admiralty Charts.

THE LOCAL PUBLIC LIBRARY, LOCAL SOCIETY LIBRARIES, AND

LOCAL MUSEUMS (see pp. 29, 63 and 72. These are likely to have map collections which will include some modern and historical maps. There may be a published catalogue or an unpublished index.

THE LOCAL RECORD OFFICE (see pp. 94-96). Historical maps and probably some modern maps will be found here. Again these may be listed in a published guide or in an unpublished index. They are likely to include estate, enclosure, tithe, public utility, and Ordnance Survey maps. If parish records have not been taken into the record office, maps, including enclosure and tithe maps, may be in the parish chest (see p. 93).

LOCAL GOVERNMENT AND LOCAL ESTATE OFFICES. Local officials such as the engineer, surveyor, town-planner and agricultural officer, and local estate offices, often have collections of maps which students may be allowed to consult.

NATIONAL AND PROVINCIAL LIBRARIES, RECORD OFFICES AND MUSEUMS. THE PUBLIC RECORD OFFICE, CHANCERY LANE, LONDON, W.C.2., and the BODLEIAN LIBRARY, OXFORD, for example, include maps in their collections. See pp. 92-101 for a list of some of the main record repositories.

THE BRITISH MUSEUM, BLOOMSBURY, LONDON, W.C.1. There is a special Map Room at the British Museum; many maps will also be found in the Department of Manuscripts. Maps include early maritime charts, historical maps of all kinds, and past and present Ordnance Survey maps, amongst which are the original drawings, usually 2 ins. to 1 ml., from which the first edition O.S. 1 in. maps were engraved. Coloured facsimiles of most of Saxton's county maps are on sale at 9s. 0d. each.

THE ROYAL GEOGRAPHICAL SOCIETY, KENSINGTON GORE, LONDON, S.W.7. The Society has a large collection of maps and atlases from the fifteenth century onwards. Reproductions of county maps by various cartographers are on sale at approximately £1 each.

INLAND REVENUE TITHE REDEMPTION OFFICE, 33-37, FINSBURY SQUARE, LONDON, E.C.2. Tithe Awards and Maps can be consulted here. A useful, free pamphlet on Tithe Records is available.

Chapter 4 Geological and Geographical Factors

Geological and geographical influences are often neglected or completely ignored in many local history studies: it would seem that the human drama has been played in a vacuum, uninfluenced by and unrelated to the particular stage on which it was performed. Even where local history is being used simply to illustrate national developments, geological and geographical factors may be significant. Thus the site of a battle or the course which it took may have been influenced by them: so, too, may the architecture of the parish church or the history of the railway. If the student is more interested in the development of the local community itself, then it is almost certain that he will need to have some knowledge of the immense potential significance of these influences and to know where to find relevant information about them.

The geological and geographical factors of which the local historian should be aware may be said to be those which constitute the physical environment of a site and its setting—rock structure, relief, drainage, climate, soil and vegetation. In thinking of their historical significance it is often impossible, so closely are they inter-related, to consider one without also referring to one or more of the others. The differing histories of the south and east of England and the north and west illustrate this point and begin to show how important such matters may be. In the former, the full force of successive invasions from the Continent has been felt, a force which diminished as the new settlers advanced northwards and westwards; witness, for example, a distribution map of Roman villas or Celtic survivals in modern Cornwall. Moreover, of the agricultural communities which predominated until recent times, those of the south-east found life easier and more comfortable, broadly speaking, than those of the north-west, a situation reflected in the distribution of population before the mid-eighteenth century. Since then, and equally significant, this distribution has changed with the progress of industrialisation. The names often given to these two regions, the Highland and Lowland Zones, emphasise only the variation in their relief. But conquerors and settlers have also been influenced by the contrasting rock types (the geologically old Highland rocks, with their thin soil cover and deposits of lead, copper and iron, compared with the cover of newer rocks, more fertile soil and relative absence of workable ore in the Lowlands); surface water supply (abundant in the north and west, more restricted in the south and east); and climate (the north wetter and windier and without the higher summer temperature of the south). All have combined in helping to produce the historical differences noted: relief affects not only the advance of armies, but also climate; rock structure and climate influence water supply as well as soil and agricultural history. The closely related nature of geological and geographical influences also quickly becomes obvious from a consideration of more local developments, such as patterns of settlement and communication within a certain area.

It is seldom appropriate, therefore, to treat these factors in isolation. Nevertheless, it may still be helpful to list each one separately and to illustrate its potential historical importance, provided that the over-simplification which this usually involves is borne in mind.

Local rocks, both the solid geology and the superficial deposits, form the first important factor. Perhaps the most significant effect of this for the historian in Britain is the close relationship which there will be in a small area between the surface geology and soils. This influence, which is discussed later, is, however, not the only one. Until the coming of the transport revolution, rock types also usually conditioned the materials from which local buildings were constructed. If a church or a stately home had to be built, bulky and expensive stone might be imported into the neighbourhood; otherwise it was quicker and cheaper to use materials which were available nearer at hand. Thus geology played a part in producing the typical, but very different, villages of Cornwall and the Cotswolds, and the eighteenth and nineteenth century local brick additions to so many towns. With the easy transport of the last hundred and fifty years, certain rocks have been generally used far beyond the localities where they occur, and we find the products of local geology, such as the ubiquitous Welsh roofing slate and the mass-produced Thames Valley brick, spreading far and wide. Besides yielding building stone, the local rocks may also have led to the growth of small or large scale industry. Tin, streamed and mined from early times in Cornwall; the iron of medieval Sussex; the coal, gravel and sand, and clay of modern England, all these spring directly from the geology.

The second point to be considered is the physical setting. This should be studied in two ways: the general position of the settlement and the precise site itself. The regional setting may reveal geographical features of far-reaching importance, a natural barrier, the Welsh highlands, for example, producing isolation; a means of communication, such as the chalk downs were for prehistoric man; or a waterway, like a river or the English Channel, which might, on different occasions, serve as both. It will also provide the essential background to local agricultural, industrial and commercial activity throughout the centuries, without which much cannot be properly understood. The settlement site itself (the original core and its subsequent growth or contraction) also merits careful investigation. What reasons, for instance, lie behind the choice of high ground for settlement? They may be partly defensive as, for example, with prehistoric hill-forts like Maiden Castle or medieval strongholds such as Corfe. Or they may be connected with water, sometimes, as with spring-line villages, ensuring an adequate water supply, sometimes, as with villages built on Fenland knolls, with the object of avoiding a surfeit. When a particular settlement is considered more closely, it will often be found that the character of building is related to relief and that, for example, in recent times higher ground has frequently been occupied by higher social classes.

The third influence which must not be overlooked is drainage. The importance of a good water supply combined with freedom from flooding has already been mentioned. Drainage may also have to be considered in relation to aspects such as the growth of villages around fords and bridges; the navigability and changing course of rivers; and the use of water power to drive mills. Water supply may also prove to have played a part in producing an agglomerated or dispersed settlement pattern, for the former often occurs in areas where surface water was not widely accessible, the latter where it was. But this is a complicated question, and a particular local pattern may well be the result of a variety of causes.

The fourth factor is climate. The general contrast which can be made between bracing and relaxing climates and their possible influence on the attitude and energy of the people who enjoy them is obvious. So, too, is the importance of its annual sunshine total to a seaside resort. Much more significant for the local historian is the study of climatic variations within a small area. Here he may be able to trace the growth of a favoured residential quarter on a healthy suburban height; there he will see a farm sited to catch all possible sunlight; while elsewhere the most profitable orchard in the parish will be the one which, for some reason he should try to investigate, escapes late frosts.

The two final influences are soil and uncultivated vegetation. It has already been suggested that local soils will, within a limited area, be in large degree the outcome of local geology: similarly, vegetation will be closely connected with soil. It will often be found that these two are amongst the most potent, as well as the most obvious, influences on local historical development. They contribute to the character of the scenery (important, for instance, in eighteenth century landscaping and for the twentieth century tourist trade) and, much more fundamental, they greatly influence the agricultural history of the community. The natural vegetation supported by different soils will have affected the date and rate of reclamation from forest, marsh and moor, and the quality of the soil will have, to a large extent, conditioned the number, size, distribution and prosperity of farms. Since the wealth of most rural communities depended, until recently, upon their agricultural potential, local soils will usually be a very important factor to consider.

These then are the major geological and geographical influences that are likely to have played a part in fashioning the local landscape and community, past and present. All local historians need constantly to be aware of their possible significance. At the same time, it should never be forgotten that, while Nature sets the stage, Man may produce unexpected scenes upon it, and may sometimes even modify the stage itself.

GENERAL BOOKS

The following is a brief selection of general works dealing with the aspects considered above:

M. Long ed., *Handbook for Geography Teachers* (5th ed., Methuen, 1964): useful lists of books and other materials on the study and teaching of geography.

J. B. Mitchell, *Historical Geography* (English Universities Press, 1954).

Sir C. Fox, *The Personality of Britain* (4th ed., Cardiff, National Museum of Wales, 1959).

H. J. Fleure, *A Natural History of Man in Britain* (Collins, 1951).

W. G. Hoskins, *The Making of the English Landscape* (Hodder and Stoughton, 1955).

F. H. Edmunds, *Geology and Ourselves* (2nd ed., Hutchinson, 1960).

J. Finberg, *Exploring Villages* (Routledge and Kegan Paul, 1958).

A. E. Smailes, *The Geography of Towns* (2nd ed., Hutchinson, 1957).

G. Manley, *Climate and the British Scene* (Collins, 1952).

C. E. P. Brooks, *Climate through the Ages* (Rev. ed., Benn, 1949).

A. E. Trueman, *Geology and Scenery in England and Wales* (Penguin Books, 1949).

J. A. Steers, *The Coastline of England and Wales* (2nd ed., Cambridge University Press, 1964).

Sir E. J. Russell, *The World of the Soil* (Collins, 1957).

A. G. Tansley, *The British Islands and their Vegetation*, 2 vols. (Cambridge University Press, 1949).

L. D. Stamp, *Man and the Land* (2nd ed., Collins, 1964).

A. Coleman and K. R. A. Maggs, *Land Use Survey Handbook* (3rd ed., Ramsgate, Isle of Thanet Geographical Association, 1962).

For detailed attempts at reconstructing selected features in past landscapes, see:

H. C. Darby ed., *The Historical Geography of England before A.D. 1800* (Cambridge University Press, 1936).

H. C. Darby ed., *The Domesday Geography of England* series (Cambridge University Press, 1952-).

Ordnance Survey, *Historical Period Maps*, above p. 39.

D. Sylvester and G. Nulty eds., *The Historical Atlas of Cheshire* (Chester, Cheshire Community Council, 1958).

MAPS AND PHOTOGRAPHS

For Ordnance Survey maps and geological, soil and land utilisation maps, see pp. 32-35. The 2½ ins., 6 ins. and 25 ins. to 1 ml. O.S. maps and the 1 in. to 1 ml. geological map are especially useful for field work relating to topics discussed in this chapter. For geological and aerial photographs, see pp. 108 and 109.

BOOKS CONTAINING MORE LOCAL INFORMATION

The beginner is likely to make most progress if he first consults maps and written descriptions and then checks and supplements this information in the field. Later he should find it more useful to work from the field back to secondary sources. The student should always walk over the area on which he is working, armed with relevant maps and with his eyes open. Vantage points, such as high ground or church towers, should be used to obtain general views. Rocks may be exposed naturally, for instance as outcrops, cliff-faces, or the sides of river valleys, or artificially, as in quarries, cuttings, trenches, pits, ditches, house-foundations and well bores. Soil profiles may be similarly exposed. C. A. Simpson, *The Study of Local Geography* (2nd ed., Methuen, 1950) and K. S. Wheeler and M. Harding eds., *Geographical Fieldwork. A Handbook* (Blond Educational, 1965) consider many aspects of field work relevant to the historian. Much field work in human geography may well be classified as field archaeology by the historian, see below, pp. 64-67.

J. Wreford Watson and J. B. Sissons, *The British Isles: a Systematic Geography* (Nelson, 1964), J. B. Mitchell ed., *Great Britain: Geographical Essays* (Cambridge University Press, 1962), and J. A. Steers, ed., *Field Studies in the British Isles* (Nelson, 1964) supply regional, and sometimes more local, information. Some areas are treated in series such as *The Face of Britain* (Batsford), *The New Naturalist* (Collins), *The Making of the English Landscape* (Hodder and Stoughton), *Regions of the British Isles* (Nelson), *Studies in Regional Planning* (Philip) and *British Landscapes through Maps* (Geographical Association), and in the British Association volumes describing the localities where its annual meetings are held. The *Victoria County History* contains a certain amount of information, but it is only recently that it has begun to treat the physical background more adequately. Detailed information relating to particular localities will often be found in the *Proceedings* of local field clubs and archaeological societies, and sometimes in specialised national periodicals such as *Geography*, the *Quarterly Journal of the Geological Society*, and the *Agricultural History Review*: for lists of articles, see *British Humanities Index: County Lists* (Library Association, 1962-, formerly *Subject Index to Periodicals*).

The Geologists' Association's *Guides* to particular areas provide useful short introductions to local geology. *Government Publications, Sectional List, no. 45* (H.M.S.O.) catalogues all the publications of the Geological Survey and Museum. Of these, the *Handbooks of the Regional Geology of Great Britain* are especially useful to the amateur. For some areas, more detailed *District Memoirs* and *Sheet Memoirs*, which accompany specific sheets of the 1 in. geological map, are available. The Geological Survey also publishes indispensable *Economic Memoirs* and *Water Supply Memoirs*. The Palaeontographical Society, *Directory of British Fossiliferous Localities* (1954) and K. M. Clayton ed., *A Bibliography of British Geomorphology* (Philip, 1964) both classify references under places. Local museums may have rock specimens, fossils and other material.

For climate, see Meteorological Office, Air Ministry, *Climatological Atlas of the British Isles* (H.M.S.O., 1952) and the *Daily* and *Monthly Weather Reports*. For soils, vegetation and agricultural history, consult B. T. Bunting ed., *An Annotated Bibliography of Memoirs and Papers on the Soils of the British Isles* (London, Geomorphological Abstracts, 1964); Land Utilisation Survey of Great Britain, *County Reports* (Geographical Publications, 1936-46) and Maps (see above, p. 35); J. T. Coppock, *An Agricultural Atlas of England and* Wales (Faber, 1964); and Royal Agricultural Society of England, *County Surveys* (1954-).

ADDRESSES

Besides the local branches of national organisations mentioned later in this section and local societies and museums, information may also be available from organisations and departments such as gas, water and electricity boards; regional headquarters of British Rail; local dock, harbour and aerodrome managers; local authority departments, for example, town planning, housing, highways and waterworks; weather stations; and county agricultural officers, farm institutes and branches of the National Farmers' Union.

THE ASSOCIATION OF AGRICULTURE, 78, BUCKINGHAM GATE, LONDON, S.W.1. promotes the interests of agriculture, publishes farm study schemes and a *Bibliography of Agricultural Source Material*, and arranges farm visits.

THE FIELD STUDIES COUNCIL, 9, DEVEREUX COURT, STRAND, LONDON, W.C.2. encourages field work. It has residential centres in various areas and publishes *Field Studies* relating to these localities.

THE FORESTRY COMMISSION, 25, SAVILE ROW, LONDON, W.1. and Deputy-Surveyors of particular forests can be consulted for information about forestry and forests.

THE GEOGRAPHICAL ASSOCIATION, 343, FULWOOD ROAD, SHEFFIELD, 10. encourages the study and teaching of geography and publishes *Geography*. There are local branches.

THE GEOLOGICAL SURVEY AND MUSEUM, EXHIBITION ROAD, SOUTH KENSINGTON, LONDON, S.W.7. publishes geological maps and books, and has an exhibition illustrating regional geology and scenery.

THE NATIONAL FEDERATION OF YOUNG FARMERS CLUBS, 55, GOWER STREET, LONDON, W.C.1. issues some useful publications. There are local branches.

THE NATIONAL PARKS COMMISSION, 1, CAMBRIDGE GATE, LONDON, N.W.1. will supply information about areas included in National Parks.

THE NATURE CONSERVANCY, 19, BELGRAVE SQUARE, LONDON, S.W.1. should be consulted for information about local nature reserves and research stations.

THE RURAL INDUSTRIES BUREAU, 35, CAMP ROAD, WIMBLEDON COMMON, LONDON, S.W.19.

THE SOIL SURVEY OF ENGLAND AND WALES, ROTHAMSTED EXPERIMENTAL STATION, HARPENDEN, HERTS. publishes *Reports* and *Memoirs*.

THE TOWN AND COUNTRY PLANNING ASSOCIATION, 28, KING STREET, COVENT GARDEN, LONDON, W.C.2. aims to improve the living and working conditions of the community, and publishes *Town and Country Planning*.

Chapter 5 Place Names

Names are given to landscape features when it becomes necessary or desirable to identify them easily or to distinguish them readily from others of the same type. Such named features include towns, villages and hamlets; natural features and fields; roads and streets; inns and houses; and churches.

The study of place names is an interesting pursuit in its own right. We may wish to know, for instance, why our settlement is called Ashby de la Zouche or Puddletown, or if there is any significance in the fact that the local church is dedicated to St. Thomas. From here it is but a short step to realising that local names incorporate a vast store of local history. Much of this has been incidentally recorded through the close association which can often be traced between a name and the object which it describes: thus, the name of a village may betray something of the natural vegetation in the neighbourhood a thousand years previously, or the name of a field or building may commemorate a former owner. Sometimes, on the other hand, as in the naming of some modern roads, particular names are deliberately bestowed in order to perpetuate the memory of an event or personality connected with national or local history. The study of names may also illuminate general problems such as population movements or aspects of language and dialect development.

Before they can be studied, names have to be collected. The student may note local names incidentally as he finds them or he may set out to collect them systematically from a variety of sources, such as books, documents, maps and people. In any particular neighbourhood there will be names which are still current and those which have fallen into disuse. Some may well be hundreds of years old, while others will be of much more recent origin.

Many names can be collected fairly easily: interpreting

their meanings correctly will usually be more difficult. It is only in this century that the study of place names has been undertaken scientifically, and many fanciful and false interpretations are still encountered. Where possible, alleged derivations should always be checked. The temptation to guess the meaning of names should also be resisted. Guessing is especially dangerous with names which originated centuries ago. The form of an old name may have altered considerably with the passage of time and, even if it has changed little, it may well not mean what it seems to suggest. Experts study the derivation of old names by collecting as many early forms as possible from Old English and medieval documents. On the basis of the elements in these early forms and in the light of their knowledge of the history of English sounds, philologists can then frequently, but not always, suggest the original form and meaning of the name. The results of these specialised investigations, as explained later, are available, and often comprehensible, to the amateur. With later names guessing is still inadvisable, and the best way of gaining some understanding of them is to keep constant watch backwards and forwards in time for links between local topography, history, and the names themselves.

TOWNS, VILLAGES AND HAMLETS

It is worth remarking that the name of a town, village or hamlet is often the earliest surviving written evidence of that settlement. Moreover, the fact that so many early names were given during periods for which written records are rare or non-existent makes them an especially valuable source of information.

A study of such names in a locality will throw light on the settlement of that region by successive invaders, since each of the major conquests of England resulted in the introduction of distinctive types of place names. The earliest names which can be attributed with certainty to particular settlers are Celtic and were given more than two thousand years ago. Some of these are names of towns, villages and hamlets but, not surprisingly, most describe impressive permanent natural features, such as rivers, hills and forests. The Celtic forms of the Latin names of Romano-British towns gave rise to the modern names of a few towns, but, where a Romano-British episode is hinted at in a place name, it is more likely to be by way of later Anglo-Saxon references to Roman remains. English names given by the Teutonic invaders and their descendants of the fifth and subsequent centuries, are very widespread. Scandinavian settlers of the ninth to eleventh centuries, Norwegians and more especially Danes, have also left their mark. By the time of the Norman Conquest the names of most of the local communities with which we are familiar to-day had been given. French names, however, were introduced during the Middle Ages and the written form and pronunciation of many established names were modified as a result of Norman-French influence. Latin additions were also made to many others. Town or village names which are of recent origin are rare.

The variety of names in a specific area and the number derived from particular influences will obviously depend upon its geographical position and its general relationship to invasion routes. Several different contributors will usually be identified, though in many localities there will probably be a preponderance of names of one type. Thus Celtic names tend to increase as one moves westwards across England and are most numerous in Cornwall and Wales; Anglo-Saxon names predominate in southern England; and Scandinavian derivations occur most frequently in areas to the north and west of Watling Street which formerly lay in the Danelaw. A combined Celtic-Norwegian contribution is evident in the north-west as a result of Irish-Norwegian immigration in the tenth century.

Place names not only yield information about the origins of early local inhabitants, but they also often reveal considerable detail of their personalities, lives, work, customs and beliefs, and of the countryside in which they dwelt. Many names incorporate an element indicating habitation or settlement, such as *Tre*rose, Southamp*ton* and Der*by*. Other elements describe aspects of the natural landscape—hills and valleys, rivers and marshes, woods and forests, trees and plants: for example, Askwith means 'ash wood', Boscombe 'box tree valley', Bromden 'broom hill', and Sherborne 'clear stream'. Another group of names indicates changes wrought by man in the countryside—woodlands cleared, roads and paths made, rivers forded and bridged: thus Thwaite signifies 'a clearing' and Morpeth 'murder path', while Highbridge is self-explanatory. There are many references to crops grown and stock raised. Personal names or descriptions of social class also often form part of a place name. The leaders of some of the earliest Saxon settlers are recorded in many names which end in *ing*, Sunna and Basa in Sonning and Basing, for instance. Innumerable individual owners, occupiers or inhabitants, both men and women, are associated through their names with a variety of features: Canfield is 'Cana's clearing' and Acton 'Acca's farmstead'. Norman family names frequently provide a distinctive addition to an original Saxon description, as, for example, in Hampton Lucy or Higham Ferrers. Kings, bishops, abbots and others are likewise commemorated, often in Latin. Other elements illustrate the paganism of the early invaders and their conversion to Christianity, or throw light on their social and legal customs.

The names of counties and their various sub-divisions, especially the hundreds or wapentakes, have similar secrets to reveal. County names fall into three groups, tribal or folk names such as Essex and Cornwall; district names like Rutland and Surrey; and those like Nottinghamshire which take their name from the chief town in the shire. A few hundreds have district names, but most are derived from local settlements or distinctive landscape features, such as hills, mounds and stones, which marked the meeting places of their hundred courts.

NATURAL FEATURES AND FIELDS

Natural features, as already seen, often figure in the names of settlements. Frequently, however, hills and valleys, rivers and streams, forests and woods, especially the smaller ones, make their own contribution to the stock of local names. Fields also have names, many of which are in danger of being lost.

The study of minor names is based on the same principles as that of place names. In many areas, the present field pattern is the result of parliamentary enclosure which occurred in the eighteenth or nineteenth century. Many names, therefore, are modern and, even where medieval names survive, they are not usually attached to the precise piece of land which they originally described. Occasionally a link with national history may be discovered in a minor name, but more usually such names will illuminate aspects of local topography and history.

A large number incorporate a word meaning 'a plot', (*croft, close, lot, yard,* or where the enclosure was for animals, *fold* or *pen*). Many describe position, size or shape (North Field, Twenty Acres, Long Close); function (*land, ridge* or *shot* for a former strip in the open arable fields, Ryeland, Hop Garden, Hoglands); or character (*brec,* 'land for cultivation', *mead,* 'meadow or pasture', Stony Ground). Nicknames are common. Some of these are complimentary in their references to productive land (Lucky, Fat, Paradise), but many more are derogatory (Lousy Close, Labour in Vain): others refer to the distant part of the parish in which they lie (America, World's End). Many names mention an owner or tenant, lay or ecclesiastical (Reeve's Plot; *glebe,* 'land belonging to the parish church for the support of the incumbent'). Useful references will often be found to local features now lost or forgotten, such as old buildings, wells or fords. Sometimes national events are also commemorated (Bunker's Hill, Waterloo).

From the evidence of names and maps it is often possible to reconstruct, at least partially, the local pattern of medieval fields.

ROADS AND STREETS

In old towns many medieval street names survive or can be traced in documents. Only a very few of these date from before 1066. Most street names are much more recent, a large number originating in the post-Industrial Revolution period of urban expansion. *Street* or *Lane* was usually used of medieval thoroughfares; *Road* is a modern introduction. Old Norse *gata*, common in Midland and northern towns, may be confusing since it means 'street' and not 'gate'.

Street and road names commonly fall into one of several groups. Many describe the character of the street (New Road, High Street, The Square); its location or direction (Above Bar Street, Poole Road); or nearby natural features (Brookside, Grove Road). A large number include the name of an important site or building (Bull Ring, Westgate Street, Church Street), and such names can sometimes be a valuable clue to a vanished landscape feature. Other names record the trades or crafts which formerly gathered thereabouts (Jewry, Tanner Street, Cooks Row). Many perpetuate the names of former owners or tenants of property in the street (French Street, Baskett's Lane), or commemorate celebrities (Shakespeare Road, Montgomery Road) or national events (Waterloo Road, Tebourba Way).

A great deal of useful work awaits local historians interested in tracing the physical growth of towns by judicious use of the evidence available in names, architecture, and maps and plans.

INNS AND HOUSES

Inns have been given names since Roman times. Some medieval, and many later, names are known or can be discovered. Some of these are still in use, but more have disappeared because inns have either been demolished or changed their names. The majority of present-day inn names in most localities are not very old.

There is such a variety of names that it is impossible to group them all significantly. A large number, however, can be described as historic and commemorative (Royal Oak, Jubilee, Marquis of Granby); heraldic and emblematic (Crown, Red Lion, Bear and Ragged Staff); and biblical and religious (Angel, Cross, Bible and Crown). Others include those concerned with natural history (Bear, Bull, Cock, Dolphin, Vine), and with trades and professions (Plough, Miners Arms, Honest Lawyer). Some are humorous, while several represent corruptions of their original names.

Much nonsense has been written about the derivation of many inn names. Standard reference works should always be consulted, and any suggested derivation of a particular name checked against what is known of local development. Usually it is wise to treat inn names as clues to possible aspects of local history rather than as proof of them. Where a name does reveal a link with history, the local use of the name may be much more recent than the event or personality commemorated.

The names of houses and other buildings may also be informative. Once again, they should generally be used as clues to follow up and check rather than as conclusive evidence.

CHURCH DEDICATIONS

The custom of dedicating churches to particular saints developed from the practice of building churches over the tombs of martyrs. The present dedication of a church can be easily ascertained from the incumbent or from the church itself. It should be remembered, however, that dedications have sometimes been changed and that accepted dedications are occasionally incorrect. The medieval dedication can be verified in various sources of which one of the most accessible is often the wills of local inhabitants which usually include a reference to the patron saint of the parish church at the time when they were made.

PERSONAL NAMES

Many surnames originated in the Middle Ages. They fall into four main groups: names derived from parents, nicknames, occupations and places. They are mentioned here because the last category is by far the largest. Some of these are derived from the names of towns and villages (Oxford, Bromley), others from minor topographical names (Attwood, Byfield). Many forenames are older than surnames. They are usually classified according to the language which produced them; for example, Julia is a Latin name and Edward is Old English.

A study of local surnames may throw light on local topography or aspects of local history such as genealogy or population movements. Forenames have phases of general popularity or unpopularity rather than great local significance though, of course, the same names often tend to be used repeatedly within the same family.

BOOKS AND ADDRESSES

K. Cameron, *English Place Names* (Batsford, 1961) and P. H. Reaney, *The Origin of English Place Names* (Routledge and Kegan Paul, 1960) are good general introductions.

E. Ekwall, *The Concise Oxford Dictionary of English Place Names* (4th ed., Oxford, Clarendon Press, 1960) briefly explains the meanings of the names of most towns and villages. A. H. Smith, *English Place Name Elements*, 2 vols. (Cambridge University Press, 1956) discusses elements alphabetically and in detail. See also E. Ekwall, *English River Names* (Oxford, Clarendon Press, 1928) and O. S. Anderson, *The English Hundred Names*, 3 vols. (Lund, Gleerup, 1934-39).

The English Place Name Society, University College, Gower Street, London, W.C.1. has published detailed surveys of the names of more than twenty counties. Other surveys are in progress: information can be obtained from the Secretary. Some counties, such as Dorset and Lancashire, have place name surveys published by individual scholars.

There are chapters on field and street names in the books by Cameron and Reaney, mentioned above. Recent Place Name Society volumes devote more space than did the early ones to minor names. W. Fraser, *Field-names in South Derbyshire* (Ipswich, Adlard and Co., 1947) and E. Ekwall, *Street Names of the City of London* (Oxford, Clarendon Press, 1954) are generally useful. The mid-nineteenth century parish Tithe Map and Award is a fruitful source of minor names.

For inn names, see J. Larwood and J. C. Hotten, *English Inn Signs* (Chatto and Windus, 1951) and W. B. Johnson, 'Some Sources of Inn History', *The Amateur Historian*, vol. vi, no. 1 (1963).

F. Bond, *Dedications and Patron Saints of English Churches* (Oxford University Press, 1914).

For personal names, see P. H. Reaney, *A Dictionary of British Surnames* (Routledge and Kegan Paul, 1958) and E. G. Withycombe, *The Oxford Dictionary of English Christian Names* (2nd ed., Oxford, Clarendon Press, 1950). On family history, see A. J. Camp, *Tracing Your Ancestors* (Foyle, 1964) and A. R. Wagner, *English Genealogy* (Oxford, Clarendon Press, 1960).

Chapter 6 Archaeological Remains

Archaeology, the study of antiquities, has been, and still often is, associated especially with the prehistoric period. This emphasis is easy to understand, for prehistoric remains are not only very old but, in the absence of written records, they also constitute the major source available for the reconstruction of that particular period. But in this century, with the increasing appreciation of the value of material remains as evidence, more and more of historic time has become the legitimate province of the archaeologist. By the outbreak of the First World War the archaeology of Roman Britain and Saxon England were recognised fields of study and, since 1945, medieval archaeology and the industrial archaeology of the eighteenth and nineteenth centuries have become well established. It is now difficult to see how any arbitrary chronological terminal date can be maintained after which, there is, as it were, no archaeological material: in such circumstances archaeology should perhaps be re-defined as 'the study of the material remains of any period in the past'.

The wealth of written records which England is fortunate to possess is a poor excuse for the frequent neglect of archaeological evidence by historians: certainly, in their work, all students of local history should be aware of the value and limitations of the evidence of material remains. Sometimes, as for the prehistoric and early historic periods, these may provide the only information which can be obtained about the locality: on other occasions, their testimony will complement, though it may not always seem to corroborate, that of other sources, particularly written records. It might be claimed that, generally speaking, archaeological material is a less conscious type of evidence than the written word and is, therefore, likely to be less biased. This is often true, but where written records are lacking it is difficult, if not impossible, to produce a detailed chronological framework and epochs are peopled with types and cultures rather than with individuals.

The material remains of the past are many and varied, and they can be classified in several ways. For present purposes a distinction will be drawn between material which is movable and that which is fixed in the landscape: both kinds will be considered in this chapter. In the next chapter, one group of fixed remains, buildings, which often form the most substantial survival from a particular period, will be discussed in more detail. This categorisation is not watertight: for example, many buildings can, if necessary, be moved, but the grouping serves as a workable introduction to the mass of material which is available.

Both movable archaeological remains and those which are fixed in the landscape occur above and beneath the ground. Some of the latter were deliberately buried; others have become covered with the passage of time. Some of the objects now above ground were once buried and are found on the surface of the earth because they have been turned up accidentally, by the action perhaps of the plough or the weather. Worked flints and coins are common examples of such discoveries. Much more of this material, however, has always been above ground level: most of the surviving tools, utensils, furniture and costumes of recent centuries fall obviously into this group.

Remains which lie underground are being increasingly revealed by deliberate archaeological excavation. While such objects may provide valuable evidence in the study of any period, they are especially important in work on prehistoric and early historic times where other types of evidence are non-existent or scarce. Since the late nineteenth century archaeological excavation has developed into a complex scientific technique as haphazard treasure-hunting has given way to the painstaking study of the typical. It is essential that unqualified amateurs, however keen, should not undertake unsupervised excavation, for, once disturbed, the stratification of a site can never be restored. For those who want to dig, facilities for training are available and many excavations where help is welcomed are now carried out annually under the direction of qualified archaeologists. Anyone eager for a specific local site to be excavated should seek expert advice. For most, however, the examination of the excavated material, together with visits to sites and the study of published reports and photographs, will provide all, and more, of the information that is needed.

MOVABLE MATERIAL

Museums are repositories of movable remains and so the student who is interested in the archaeology of his neighbourhood should, early in his investigation, make himself familiar with their resources.

Local museums vary enormously in size and scope and in the extent to which they emphasise the immediate locality in their work. But wherever he is, the enquirer is likely to find a local, county or regional museum, and often more than one, relevant to his interests. The least rewarding localities in this respect will be those areas where there is no county museum and where local government restrictions have prevented nearby town museums from concerning themselves with the history of those districts. Not only do the contents of local museums represent ready-to-use collections of movable material remains, but it is also probable that the curators and their staff will be able to give advice and assistance about other aspects of local archaeology. They will probably have additional material which is not displayed, as well perhaps, as maps, books, topographical and subject card-indexes, and other aids, all of which may be made available on request. They may also know of appropriate material in other museums and in private collections.

The exhibits displayed in local museums are usually arranged chronologically, by topics, or by both methods, and a quick examination of them often forms a useful introduction to many aspects of local study and to the kinds of objects which are likely to be encountered in a particular kind of enquiry. Thus, individual sections of many museums are devoted to specific periods from prehistory to the nineteenth century, while others illustrate themes such as weapons, crafts, coins, costume, furniture, or a local industry. A few places, like Bristol, Leicester and York, have attractive folk museums which reconstruct aspects of past local life from material remains, and it is unfortunate that such institutions have not been more widely established.

National museums also often contain material relating to a locality. Some of them, the British Museum, for example, are general repositories. Others are more specialised: with these, their names, such as the Museum of English Rural Life at Reading, or the National Maritime Museum at Greenwich, usually indicate the nature of their special collections.

Further material, the variety of which defies description, may also be discovered in private ownership. Some of these objects will be treasured, but relatively insignificant; a few coins or pieces of pottery from an old excavation, for example. Other items, such as many rural bygones, have an interest of which their owners are very often unaware. Much of this material may well be lost or destroyed if local investigators do not interest themselves in it. To record or gather it they will need strong legs (for walking is the only way in which the neighbourhood can be explored in detail), and observant eyes. Building sites, drainage trenches, ploughed land and rabbit burrows, as well as homes, yards, workshops and factories, may all yield valuable clues or finds. The exact site of any discovery should always be carefully recorded.

FIELD REMAINS

The qualities of energy and observation are even more necessary in identifying and studying the other major group of material remains in the locality, those which are fixed in the landscape. A few of these, the footings of a Roman villa or a medieval cottage, for instance, may have been exposed by digging, but the essential characteristic of field archaeology as a study is that it is concerned with landscape features and does not involve excavation. Unlike excavation, therefore, there is no risk that evidence may be destroyed: indeed, by producing descriptions, measured drawings and photographs the amateur can often add to existing knowledge. He may do this by detailed work on already well known sites and monuments, and the main purpose of this description is to draw attention to known remains. But, so neglected has much of this type of material been, that he also stands a good chance of discovering new sites. For this work medium and large scale Ordnance Survey maps will be needed. These indicate, in distinctive types for prehistoric, Romano-British and post-Roman antiquities, many known sites and finds, and also enable new discoveries to be plotted.

Field remains in the landscape can be conveniently considered here in six broad groups: another group, consisting of most buildings and those ruins which are usually considered to be of architectural interest, is described in the next chapter. The remains in these six categories are connected with habitation sites, agriculture, industrial workings, religious life, communications and, finally, miscellaneous activities. The number and character of the sites and monuments which will be found in any particular locality will, like the movable objects, depend upon a variety of factors. Different remains are likely to exist in a lowland parish from those which will be found in a highland area. In the north and west, sites with military significance are more plentiful than they are in the south and east. In a heavily urbanised area most signs of ancient activity may have been swept away, but there may be an abundance of more recent relics by way of compensation.

Prehistoric habitation sites may be revealed in caves and shelters, in scanty clues to huts and farms, or in impressive hill forts. These, like Roman remains, such as villas, urban buildings and defences, have frequently been studied in detail. It is only recently, however, that most aspects of medieval settlement, other than large castles and ecclesiastical buildings, have begun to attract attention. The mottes of small castles, the sites of moated homesteads, the boundaries of parks, and the remains of deserted, medieval villages may well be discovered, some of them hitherto unrecognised and unrecorded.

The landscape of rural England is to a large extent the product of man's reclamation and cultivation of the land over the centuries. Where subsequent intensive ploughing has not taken place, signs of prehistoric or Romano-British agriculture may be found in field patterns of different kinds, their variety depending largely on the types of plough which were used. Vestiges of the medieval open field system are common. Very exceptionally, open arable field strips are still cultivated: more usually, there are indications that they may lie ossified in a locality. Thus the long terrace-like lynchets which are often found following the contours of chalk downs and the undulating ridge and furrow pattern encountered in many Midlands fields both frequently, but not always, betray the former existence of such cultivation. Extensive areas of common land, often the remains of the common pasture or waste of the medieval community, abound, and marlpits where fertiliser was dug and pounds for stray beasts also survive. Modern field patterns are likely to contain many clues to reclamation and agricultural history. The small fields of Cornwall with their network of winding lanes, for example, suggest early enclosure, in contrast to the larger and more regular hedged fields, served by straight roads, of the Midlands and East Anglia where the effects of parliamentary enclosure in the eighteenth and nineteenth centuries are most evident. In towns, streets often follow earlier boundaries of agricultural importance.

The remains of industrial activity which may be discovered again range widely over the centuries. Without written evidence it may often be difficult to decide when some of them flourished, for stone and slate quarrying, metal working, pot and tile making, saltings, marl and lime digging, and charcoal burning, to quote some examples, usually leave behind few datable remains. Buildings associated with industries, both pre- and post-Industrial Revolution, are discussed later: ruinous buildings and derelict machinery, however, are archaeological remains which deserve investigation.

Probably some of the best known field remains to the amateur are those of a religious nature, such as prehistoric earth, wood and stone circles, standing stones, and stone rows and avenues. Sculptured Celtic crosses, holy wells, and memorial pillars which are common in the Highland Zone, have also been extensively studied. Most widespread of all are burial mounds. These are of various types, including Neolithic long, and Bronze Age round, barrows, as well as mounds from the early historic periods. The graves and headstones of more recent centuries also repay investigation, both for the light they may throw on local craftsmanship and for their information about local inhabitants.

Prehistoric tracks, Roman roads, medieval streets, drove roads and lanes, enclosure and turnpike roads, and modern bypasses and motorways may have affected the development of a locality and left their mark in the landscape. Besides the roads themselves, details like milestones, signposts, toll houses, pavements, street lighting and traffic signs may well repay study. Canals, perhaps Roman or medieval, but dating more probably from the late eighteenth or early nineteenth century, may also exist, implying that there may be locks, tunnels, towpaths, cottages or inns to be found. In many areas the building of railways had a profound effect on the local scene. Vast cuttings and embankments were made, tunnels were excavated, and bridges were thrown across roads and rivers. Time has healed many of the scars, but there is still much to study, including an increasing number of abandoned lines. The pattern of local communications, the relationship of routes to relief, the places linked and the places avoided should also be considered.

The group of miscellaneous remains cannot be described in general terms. Their variety is perhaps indicated by mentioning that one published list of them opens with 'animals' doors', includes 'bee-boles, decoy ponds, hill figures, mazes, plague pits and stocks' and ends with 'weather vanes'.

Finally, there have been erected many monuments, memorials and commemorative or informative plaques which give details about the site or feature to which they are attached. These are too often overlooked, for they can, especially in large towns, form a valuable introduction to local study.

GENERAL BOOKS

S. Piggott, *Approach to Archaeology* (Black, 1960) is an interesting introduction to the subject. The Council for British Archaeology has published *British Archaeology: a Booklist* (The Council, 1960) especially for teachers.

J. Hawkes, *Discovering the Past* (Rev. ed., National Council of Social Service, 1956) is a brief pamphlet dealing with surface finds. See also Royal Commission on Historical Monuments (England), *A Matter of Time: an Archaeological Survey of the River Gravels of England* (H.M.S.O., 1960).

R. L. S. Bruce Mitford ed., *Recent Archaeological Excavations in Great Britain* (Routledge and Kegan Paul, 1956) and the *Reports* of the Research Committee of the Society of Antiquaries (1913-) describe important excavations. G. Webster, *Practical Archaeology* (Black, 1963) is one of several introductions to digging.

It is impossible to list here many books which deal with particular movable remains. But see museum publications; for example, the British Museum *Guides* to the antiquities of various periods, the London Museum, *Catalogue*, and the Victoria and Albert Museum booklets on *Furniture, Silver*, etc.; M. and C. H. B. Quennell, *A History of Everyday Things in England, 1066-1914*, 4 vols. (Several eds., Batsford); G. C. Brooke, *English Coins from the Seventh Century to the Present Day* (3rd ed., Methuen, 1955); R. E. Oakeshott, *The Archaeology of Weapons* (Lutterworth Press, 1960); F. M. Kelly and R. Schwabe, *A Short History of Costume and Armour, 1066-1800*, 2 vols. (Batsford, 1931); and D. Yarwood, *The English Home: a Thousand Years of Furnishing and Decoration* (Batsford, 1956). The C.B.A. booklist, *British Archaeology* supplies many additional references.

Field remains are difficult to group. Above, they have been broadly classified by type. Some books follow this arrangement, others group them by period. E. S. Wood, *A Field Guide to Archaeology* (Collins, 1963) and W. G. Hoskins, *The Making of the English Landscape* (Hodder and Stoughton, 1955) are invaluable general surveys. See also Ordnance Survey, *Field Archaeology: Some Notes for Beginners* (4th ed., H.M.S.O., 1963); O. G. S. Crawford, *Archaeology in the Field* (Phoenix House, 1953); and M. W. Beresford, *History on the Ground* (Lutterworth Press, 1957). More detailed introductions to the remains of special periods are S. Thomas, *Pre-Roman Britain* (Studio Vista, 1965); L. Cottrell, *Seeing Roman Britain* (Bell, 1957); and D. Wilson, *The Anglo-Saxons* (Thames and Hudson, 1960). The archaeology of later periods is covered in books on topics rather than on chronological periods: Wood, *Field Guide to Archaeology* has a useful bibliography. A few titles are listed here in the order in which field remains have been described.

M. W. Beresford, *The Lost Villages of England* (Lutterworth Press, 1954).

J. Higgs, *The Land* (Studio Vista, 1964); H. C. Bowen, *Ancient Fields* (British Association, 1961); C. S. and C. S. Orwin, *The Open Fields* (2nd ed., Oxford, Clarendon Press, 1954); W. G. Hoskins and L. D. Stamp, *The Common Lands of England and Wales* (Collins, 1963); and H. C. Prince, 'Parkland in the English Landscape', *The Amateur Historian*, vol. iii, no. 8 and vol. iv, no. 1 (1958).

C. J. Singer, E. J. Holmyard and A. R. Hall eds., *A History of Technology*, 5 vols. (Oxford University Press, 1954-58); K. Hudson, *Industrial Archaeology* (Barker, 1963); and two books by J. P. M. Pannell, *Techniques of Industrial Archaeology* (Dawlish, David and Charles, 1966) and *An Illustrated History of Civil Engineering* (Thames and Hudson, 1964).

L. V. Grinsell, *The Ancient Burial Mounds of England* (2nd ed., Methuen, 1953) and F. Burgess, *English Churchyard Memorials* (Lutterworth Press, 1964).

J. Simmons, *Transport* (Vista Books, 1962); H. W. Timperley and E. Brill, *Ancient Trackways of Wessex* (Phoenix House, 1965); I. D. Margary, *Roman Roads in Britain*, 2 vols. (Phoenix House, 1955-57); E. Jervoise, *Ancient Bridges of England and Wales*, 4 vols. (Architectural Press, 1930-36); C. Hadfield, *British Canals* (Rev. ed., Phoenix House, 1959); D. St. J. Thomas and C. R. Clinker eds., *A Regional History of the Railways of Great Britain*, 4 vols. to date (Phoenix House, 1960-); F. E. Wilson, *The British Tram* (Marshall, 1961); L. T. C. Rolt, *Motoring History* (Studio Vista, 1964); and the *Journal of Transport History*.

M. Marples, *White Horses and Other Hill Figures* (Country Life, 1949); A. H. Burne, *The Battlefields of England* (2nd ed.,

Methuen, 1951) and *More Battlefields of England* (Methuen, 1952); W. Cunningham, *Monuments of English Municipal Life* (S.P.C.K., 1920); and O. G. S. Crawford, 'Place Names and Archaeology' in A. Mawer and F. M. Stenton eds., *Introduction to the Survey of English Place Names* (Cambridge University Press, 1924).

MAPS AND PICTORIAL RECORDS

Ordnance Surveys maps should be consulted: see pp. 32-42. Modern maps, especially those on the scale of 2½ ins., 6 ins. and 25 ins. to 1 ml., incorporate a great deal of archaeological information. Historical Period Maps and their accompanying booklets are valuable. The Archaeological Branch of the Ordnance Survey is compiling card-indexes of objects of archaeological interest covering the prehistoric and historic periods. There are subject and topographical indexes, subdivided by counties. These can be consulted by arrangement with the Director General at Maybush, Southampton, where the cards are housed. A local museum or society may have 6 in. maps with this, and additional, information added. For photographs and pictures see pp. 108-109.

BOOKS CONTAINING MORE LOCAL INFORMATION

Much of the information in this section applies also to 'Buildings' (see pp. 74-86). Some of the general works listed above contain local material.

A. Fellows, *England and Wales: a Traveller's Companion* (Oxford, Clarendon Press, 1964) is a useful introduction to archaeology and buildings with lists of sites and museums. There are similar lists in Wood, *Field Guide to Archaeology.*

For area lists of prehistoric and Roman remains, see N. Thomas, *A Guide to Prehistoric England* (Batsford, 1960) and J. Hawkes, *A Guide to the Prehistoric and Roman Monuments in England and Wales* (Chatto and Windus, 1951). The former is preparing a similar volume on Roman Britain.

Sectional List no. 27, Ancient Monuments and Historic Buildings (H.M.S.O.) gives details of Ministry of Works publications. These include *Ancient Monuments and Historic Buildings in the Care of the Ministry of Works, Open to the Public* (2nd ed., H.M.S.O., 1963) and, for England, three short authoritative *Illustrated Regional Guides to Ancient Monuments in the Ownership or Guardianship of the Ministry of Works* entitled *Northern England, Southern England* and *East Anglia and the Midlands.* These are general surveys which give details of access to particular sites: *Official Guides to Ancient Monuments and Historic Buildings* are catalogued in *Sectional List* 27. A *List of Ancient Monuments in England and Wales* with *Supplements* is published.

Sectional List 27 also enumerates the valuable county *Inventories* of the Royal Commission on Historical Monuments (England). These describe earthworks, sites and monuments under parishes, and are very well illustrated. Originally no remains later than 1714 were included but, for recent volumes, the date has been advanced to 1851. Volumes have been published for some eleven counties. The Commission has an extensive card-index and photographic collection which can be consulted by arrangement.

For publications concerning National Trust properties and other houses which contain information on interiors and furniture, see p. 84.

The *County Archaeologies* (Methuen, 1930-), covering Berkshire, Cornwall, Kent, Middlesex and London, Somerset, Surrey, Sussex and Yorkshire from earliest times to 1066, are still valuable. Volumes in the more recent *Ancient Peoples and Places* series (Thames and Hudson) and the *Regional Archaeologies* series (Cory, Adams and Mackay) which is designed to cover the British Isles, are very useful. K. Hudson, *The Industrial Archaeology of Southern England* (Dawlish, David and Charles, 1965) and D. Smith, *The Industrial Archaeology of the East Midlands* (1965) are the first volumes in a projected series. A detailed regional survey may be available such as Sir C. Fox, *The Archaeology of the Cambridge Region* (Cambridge University Press, 1923); L. V. Grinsell, *The Archaeology of Wessex* (Methuen, 1958) or G. Copley, *An Archaeology of South-East England* (Phoenix House, 1958). There are useful regional bibliographies in the C. B. A. *British Archaeology: a*

Booklist: see also its annual *Archaeological Bibliography for Great Britain and Ireland.*

If the *Victoria County History* has been published, it will contain much information. In the older volumes, the chapters on 'Early Man', 'Earthworks', 'Romano-British Remains', 'Anglo-Saxon Remains' and 'Architecture' should be consulted. Some of the information may be out of date, and some topics of current interest will not be covered. The plan of presenting archaeological material has changed in some more recent volumes: for example, Wiltshire has an *Archaeological Gazetteer.*

The *Proceedings* of local archaeological, architectural and field clubs are likely to be fruitful sources. Many national journals, published by specialist societies, contain references to archaeological sites and discoveries. The most useful are *Antiquaries' Journal, Antiquity, Archaeologia, Archaeological Journal, Journal of the British Archaeological Association, Archaeological News Letter,* and *Journal of Industrial Archaeology.* For special periods, see *Proceedings of the Prehistoric Society, Journal of Roman Studies* and *Medieval Archaeology.* The last two include annual surveys of current work in different parts of the country. The *Gentleman's Magazine* is worth consulting for discoveries in the nineteenth century, and early files of newspapers often include otherwise unpublished information.

ADDRESSES

For the addresses and brief descriptions of local and national museums, see *Museums and Galleries in Great Britain and Ireland* (Index Publishers, annually) and *Guide to London Museums and Galleries* (H.M.S.O.). Some members of the staff of local libraries and planning departments are also very knowledgeable about local remains.

THE COUNCIL FOR BRITISH ARCHAEOLOGY, 4, ST. ANDREW'S PLACE, LONDON, N.W.1. will supply details of its regional organisations and their activities. It publishes various material including a list of forthcoming excavations where help is needed.

THE MINISTRY OF PUBLIC BUILDING AND WORKS, LAMBETH BRIDGE HOUSE, ALBERT EMBANKMENT, LONDON, S.E.1. may be able to supply additional information about sites in its care.

THE ROYAL COMMISSION ON HISTORICAL MONUMENTS (ENGLAND), FIELDEN HOUSE, GREAT COLLEGE STREET, LONDON, S.W.1. has card-indexes and photographs which can be consulted by arrangement.

There are many useful specialist societies. Their names indicate their interests, and most publish a journal. These include, in addition to those already mentioned:

THE BRITISH NUMISMATIC SOCIETY, DEPARTMENT OF COINS AND MEDALS, BRITISH MUSEUM, LONDON, W.C.1.

THE ARMS AND ARMOUR SOCIETY, 40, GREAT JAMES STREET, HOLBORN, LONDON, W.C.1.

THE DESERTED MEDIEVAL VILLAGE RESEARCH GROUP, 67, GLOUCESTER CRESCENT, LONDON, N.W.1.

THE BRITISH AGRICULTURAL HISTORY SOCIETY, DEPARTMENT OF ECONOMIC HISTORY, THE UNIVERSITY, EXETER.

THE NEWCOMEN SOCIETY FOR THE STUDY OF THE HISTORY OF ENGINEERING AND TECHNOLOGY, SCIENCE MUSEUM, SOUTH KENSINGTON, LONDON, S.W.7.

THE NATIONAL MARITIME MUSEUM, GREENWICH, LONDON, S.E.10. for maritime archaeology.

THE RAILWAY AND CANAL HISTORICAL SOCIETY, 26, CLARENCE STREET, ULVERSTON, LANCS.

THE OMNIBUS SOCIETY, EROS HOUSE, 111, BAKER STREET, LONDON, W.1.

Chapter 7 Buildings

Cursory perusal of a random selection of published histories quickly reveals the way in which the study of buildings has usually been approached by English local historians. Often, despite the rich variety of buildings which most areas enjoy, they are not mentioned at all. When they are, one or two buildings, which by implication are regarded as more important than the others, are usually singled out for description. These are likely to be old, and they will almost certainly be studied in isolation, without regard to other buildings in the neighbourhood and frequently with little reference to others of similar type elsewhere. Nearly always, ecclesiastical structures, especially medieval churches and religious houses, receive most attention: castles and country houses are also likely to be described. Aesthetic appeal is a prime consideration and the details of architectural style are often discussed at great length. This kind of attitude to the study of buildings closely resembles the early nineteenth century approach to archaeology: the spirit is that of the treasure-hunt and energy is concentrated on the extraordinary remains of an artificially and arbitrarily limited period which are too often studied as dead antiquities and not for what they may also reveal of their original selves and their once living owners or occupiers.

Recently, some historians have begun to study more kinds of buildings and to ask different questions about buildings in general. There is a vast amount of work in all areas awaiting local historians who will follow their lead. Some such work, on ruined or partially ruined buildings, for example, resembles the study of remains described in the previous chapter as archaeological. Other aspects could well be classified as human geography. But all form a part of, and illuminate, local history, especially social and economic developments. The particular problems to be solved in a specific locality will, of course, vary with the number, age, style and function of the local buildings which will themselves be the outcome of interrelated factors. Nevertheless, wherever it is undertaken, there is likely to be a sense of urgency about much of this work because of the rapid rate at which buildings are now being altered or destroyed.

GROUPS OF BUILDINGS

The student's first need is to appreciate the importance and value of looking broadly at the built-up areas and the open spaces in his neighbourhood. The general pattern of settlement and the distribution of buildings of particular ages and types must be considered and, if possible, explained. The characteristics which give a place its peculiar look must be identified and an attempt made to unravel the geographical, historical and architectural strands in its make-up. The face of a settlement often epitomises the past and present life of the local community and prompts innumerable lines of enquiry, such as the periods at which the place has been prosperous or in decline, the basis of its economic activity, and the influence of foreign settlers. A great deal may be observed and learned from certain vantage points like hills, cross-roads and towers, and from similar views supplied by maps and aerial photographs. The area should also be walked over, first in order to gain general impressions and then to make a detailed survey of the aspects which are relevant to any particular investigation which is being undertaken. On different occasions, for example, general land utilisation, building periods, styles or materials, or classification by function might be the immediate concern.

Locating the original site or sites from which the local community has developed and explaining the shape of the present settlement are topics of fundamental interest and importance. Where was the earliest inhabited spot? Who chose it? And why? Food, water, defence and shelter were vital necessities for early settlers and many sites reveal the influence of these factors. Thus the presence of a spring or well, a river confluence or loop, dry ground above a flood-plain, a ford or bridge, a gentle slope, good farming land, cross-roads, a harbour, a castle, an abbey, or an industrial establishment, will often be significant, Once established, how and when did the settlement grow to its present size? Does it possess a recognizable shape? For example, some villages are compact, others are scattered; some line a main road, others surround a square or village green. What reasons lie behind the evolution of a particular pattern? The physical shape of a town is also the outcome of a variety of geographical and historical influences. The nature of the underlying rocks, variations in relief and accidents of land-ownership, for instance, are often important. So are Roman, medieval, or later, town walls which frequently affect the shape of a settlement long after they have ceased to perform their original military function. Vestiges of the former town fields may also be seen: sometimes portions remain as open spaces in the modern urban scene; more often some of their pattern is delineated in the street plan of the built-up area which now covers them. On many occasions the architectural style of a suburb provides a valuable clue to the period at which that part of the town developed. It should also be remembered that centres of settlement change and what was once the hub of a town's activity may now be a backwater. Furthermore, a former thriving community, urban or rural, may now be completely dead, and its site abandoned. Large numbers of deserted medieval villages, for example, have been identified in recent years.

The effect of deliberate planning on settlement shape is another influence which should not be overlooked. Traces of the planned towns which resulted from the borough fever of the twelfth and thirteenth centuries are not uncommon, though they are less well known than Georgian attempts at urban design. Modern town and country planning makes a more general positive contribution to settlement shapes, but it also frequently alters traditional patterns drastically by the ease with which it is able to disregard long-established boundaries.

INDIVIDUAL BUILDINGS

The policy advocated for the study of groups of buildings, that of looking at them as organic wholes, should also be adopted in the consideration of individual buildings and ruins.

Certain general principles can be fruitfully applied in the investigation of buildings of all kinds. Few structures can be examined in detail without the co-operation of the owner or custodian, so that it is wise, where necessary, to seek permission and enlist help. The general setting of a building should always be studied first. The site, the reasons for its choice, the name, if it has one, the grounds, and any outbuildings, all these points need to be considered. Then, before rushing inside, the investigator should carefully examine the building itself from without. What general impression does it convey? Is it large or small, old or new, attractive or unattractive? Why was it erected? What purposes were it, and its several parts, intended to serve? Has it, with the passage of time, continued to perform its original function? If not, in what ways, if at all, has it been altered to meet its new purpose? From the outside the shape of the place and something of its plan can be detected. Often the back of a building has been less altered than the front. Clues to its growth in the form of blocked windows and doorways and major variations of wall thickness, floor level and roof line are also readily apparent.

Dating a building, or its parts if it has grown piecemeal, is often difficult. Date stones which are common as foundation or head-stones may help, but they can also mislead. The use of particular architectural styles can be informative, though it is necessary to know when such styles were employed locally rather than rely on a text-book definition of the period during which they were generally in use. Local stylistic details, such as the size and pattern of chimneys, are sometimes a more reliable guide. The degree of weathering can be helpful, in distinguishing, for instance, between original and nineteenth century Church Gothic.

While the materials used in the construction of the main

fabric are not always visible from outside a building, they often are. These need to be identified and the reasons for their use in walls and roof considered. Local materials—timber, stone, flint, cob, brick, thatch—should be seen especially in relation to local geology. The origin, transport and payment for imported materials may also be worth pursuing. Such investigations lead on to others. How far was a particular builder limited or given structural or ornamental opportunities by the materials at his disposal? To what extent did his knowledge of architectural principles enable him to overcome any restrictions imposed by them? How far did fashion or taste dictate what he should do?

The same kind of approach should be followed in studying the interior of a building as suggested for the exterior: the general structure and then the detail should be noted and, as far as possible, explained. All floors need to be examined.

The best way to begin to understand buildings is to make records of them. Elevations of each side and scale plans of each floor should be attempted, with accompanying notes, sketches and photographs. Important exterior points to be covered include materials, type of roof, chimney stack, number and position of doors and windows, and architectural details and decoration. Inside, the method of construction and the distribution and lay-out of rooms should be recorded, and the available services listed. The position of staircases, passages, doors and windows, as well as changes in wall position and thickness and floor level, may be very significant. The oldest parts of a building are frequently found in a cellar or inside the roof.

The study of those types of local buildings which usually attract some attention will be enlivened if the method described above is adopted. Cathedrals, religious houses, parish churches, castles, country houses and almshouses will no longer be seen solely or predominantly as collections of beautiful architectural details, but also as organic units which provide illustrations of both building developments and social and economic history. For example, the changes in castle construction are seen to be the result of the relative importance, at different times, of defence and comfort, and ruins, such as those of religious houses, become easier to understand once it is appreciated that functional aspects of life and liturgy produced a common basic plan. The study of the parish church is also transformed as changes in structure and style are related to economic, social and religious developments.

It is also very necessary to extend this same interest and spirit to many kinds of buildings which the local historian too often neglects. Lesser domestic architecture provides an important example. The use of cruck or timber frame, the introduction of the load-bearing wall, the variety of materials and the influence of the transport revolution, the purpose served by different parts, the aping of fashion, and the effect of sanitary standards on design and lay-out, are among the aspects which should receive attention in any survey of housing development. Other types of building which well repay investigation include denominational chapels, industrial and commercial structures, and those connected with transport and communication. Mills, mines, workshops, factories, warehouses, public utility undertakings, civic buildings, schools, shops, railway stations and garages illustrate the variety of opportunity. That many of these buildings date only from Victorian or later days is no excuse whatsoever for the customary practice of either ignoring them altogether or simply bemoaning their existence.

HERALDRY

Many buildings incorporate valuable evidence in the form of heraldic emblems and devices. These may be found, for example, on roof bosses, wood carvings, stained and painted glass, tombs and hatchments in churches; on panels, lintels and glass in private houses; and on public buildings such as town halls, hospitals and schools. Heraldry developed in the Middle Ages in the adoption of devices on their shields by the knights of western Europe. Later, these arms were also borne on seals and tombs. A Heralds' College, which is still in existence, was established in 1485 to control the bearing of arms. The interpretation of heraldic symbols is not always easy, but there are several handbooks on the subject.

BOUNDARIES

A variety of boundaries will be encountered in the study of settlements and individual buildings. These, perhaps intimately linked with local life for a thousand years or more, often throw light on local history. A few major earthworks, such as the Wansdyke and Offa's Dyke, and some county boundaries, have been studied in connection with conquest, settlement and landownership in Saxon and early medieval England. But, generally speaking, boundaries have not attracted much attention.

The bounds of old ecclesiastical parishes should be investigated on the map and on the ground, and note taken of natural features followed or ignored, banks and ditches constructed, and street patterns outlined. The size of some parishes may contrast sharply with that of others near at hand. Often the agricultural potential of the locality was a significant factor determining this contrast: where the soil is fertile, parishes tend to be smaller. The shape of a parish may be governed by the same reason: in many downland valleys, for instance, the boundaries form rectangles running from the river to the crest of the downs so as to incorporate, for early farmers, meadow, arable and pasture. Changes in parish boundaries should be traced and accounted for, and the relationship of manorial and modern civil and ecclesiastical parish boundaries to those of the old ecclesiastical parish should be established and, if possible, explained. Modern field boundaries may still tell the story of medieval reclamation from the waste or indicate, here and there, the medieval pattern of strip cultivation. The common fields may also have left their mark in towns, in the broad pattern of built-up areas or in street plans. The boundaries of individual holdings may be just as interesting to study. Many are old, and many apparently recent ones perpetuate earlier bounds. Modern large scale planning, with its wholesale reconstruction of town centres and building of motorways, is already destroying invaluable evidence on the ground and, if this kind of work is not undertaken soon, much of it will have to be done, much less interestingly in the future, from written records alone.

GENERAL BOOKS

For the sites, shapes, growth and characters of villages and towns, see T. Sharp, *The Anatomy of the Village* (Penguin Books, 1946) and G. Martin, *The Town* (Vista Books, 1961) in addition to books mentioned on pp. 47-48. Visual aspects of modern developments are considered in G. Cullen, *Townscape* (Architectural Press, 1962) and E. Johns, *British Townscapes* (Ed. Arnold, 1965).

Books on the various architectural styles are listed in bibliographies such as R.I.B.A., *Architecture. A List of Books for Schools* (The Institute, 1962), and in the volumes in the Oxford and Pelican *History of Art* series. D. Yarwood, *The Architecture of England* (Batsford, 1963), C. Trent, *England in Brick and Stone* (Anthony Blond, 1958), and E. Vale, *How to Look at Old Buildings* (2nd ed., Batsford, 1946) are useful general works.

A. Clifton Taylor, *The Pattern of English Building* (2nd ed., Batsford, 1965) is the best book on materials, methods and styles: see also N. Davey, *A History of Building Materials* (Phoenix House, 1961), T. D. Atkinson, *Local Style in English Architecture* (Batsford, 1947) and L. F. Salzman, *Building in England down to 1540* (Oxford, Clarendon Press, 1952).

Among the many books on religious houses, see R. Gilyard-Beer, *Abbeys* (H.M.S.O., 1959) and several books by G. H. Cook, *English Monasteries in the Middle Ages* (Phoenix House, 1961), *The English Cathedral through the Centuries* (Phoenix House, 1957), *English Collegiate Churches of the Middle Ages* (Phoenix House, 1959), and *Medieval Chantries and Chantry Chapels* (Rev. ed., Phoenix House, 1963): all have bibliographies.

A. Savidge, *The Parsonage in England: its History and Architecture* (S.P.C.K., 1964) and W. H. Godfrey, *The English Almshouse* (Faber, 1955).

There are various guides to the study of the parish church: A. Needham, *How to Study an Old Church* (3rd ed., Batsford, 1948) and M. D. Anderson, *Looking for History in British Churches* (Murray, 1951) are among the most useful to the beginner. A. Hamilton Thompson, *The Historical Growth of the English Parish Church* (Cambridge University Press, 1911) and G. W. O. Addleshaw and F. Etchells, *The Architectural Setting of Anglican Worship* (Faber, 1948) deal with the structure of the church. F. H. Crossley, *English Church Design, A.D. 1040-1540* (Batsford, 1945); F. H. Crossley, *English Church Craftsmanship* (Batsford, 1941); and J. C. Cox and A. Harvey, *English Church Furniture, Fittings and Accessories* (Methuen, 1907) introduce some of its details. There are countless books on its architecture, furniture and fittings including specialised works on subjects like mural paintings, stained glass, fonts, and church plate. Tombs and monuments are often of special interest to the local historian: see F. H. Crossley, *English Church Monuments, A.D. 1150-1550* (Batsford, 1921); K. A. Esdaile, *English Church Monuments, 1510-1840* (Batsford, 1946); and M. Stephenson, *List of Monumental Brasses in the British Isles, and Supplement* (Headley Bros., 1926-38).

B. H. St. J. O'Neil, *Castles* (H.M.S.O., 1953) and R. A. Brown, *English Castles* (Batsford, 1962) are short, authoritative introductions. For country houses, see R. Dutton, *The English Country House* (Rev. ed., Batsford, 1962) and the *English Country House* series (Country Life).

M. W. Barley, *The House and Home* (Vista Books, 1963) and A. Henderson, *The Family House in England* (Phoenix House, 1964) introduce the subject and its literature. M. Wood, *The English Medieval House* (Phoenix House, 1965) is a detailed study. M. W. Barley, *The English Farmhouse and Cottage* (Routledge and Kegan Paul, 1961) discusses their development and regional variations. R. B. Wood-Jones, *Traditional Domestic Architecture in the Banbury Region* (Manchester University Press, 1964) is planned as the first of a series.

Industrial building is considered generally in W. H. Chaloner and A. E. Musson, *Industry and Technology* (Vista

Books, 1963) and in specialised works such as R. Wailes, *The English Windmill* (Routledge and Kegan Paul, 1954); L. Syson, *British Water Mills* (Batsford, 1965); and C. L. V. Meeks, *The Railway Station* (Architectural Press, 1959).

C. Boutell, rev. C. W. Scott Giles and J. P. Brooke-Little, *Heraldry* (Rev. ed., Warne, 1966) and C. W. Scott Giles, *The Romance of Heraldry* (Dent, 1965) are standard introductions. Of direct practical value are J. and J. B. Burke, *A General Armory of England, Scotland and Ireland* (3rd. ed., Bohn, 1844) and J. W. Papworth and A. W. Morant, *Ordinary of British Armorials* (1874: reprinted Tabard Publications, 1961). The former permits the tracing of arms when the family is known, the latter reverses the process.

MAPS AND PICTORIAL RECORDS

For modern and historical maps, see pp. 32-42, and for pictorial records, pp. 104-109.

BOOKS CONTAINING MORE LOCAL INFORMATION

Some of the general books just listed contain local material. The maps, the field and several of the books mentioned under 'Archaeology' on pp. 67-72 are relevant: see especially, but not solely, A. Fellows, *England and Wales: a Traveller's Companion* (Oxford, Clarendon Press, 1964); *Sectional List no. 27, Ancient Monuments and Historic Buildings* (H.M.S.O.) and the publications which it lists; and the *Inventories* of the Royal Commission on Historical Monuments (England).

Several series have individual volumes on many counties. N. Pevsner, *The Buildings of England* (Penguin Books, 1951-) series, which discusses buildings of all types and dates, is often the most stimulating. Fewer have been published in the *Architectural Guides* (Murray) and the *Shell Guides* (Faber) series, but they are useful. A more traditional approach to architecture is employed in the *Little Guides* (Methuen) and the *Queen's England* series (Hodder and Stoughton). For London, there are now more than thirty volumes in the valuable *Survey of London* which records public and private buildings of some historical or architectural merit built before 1900.

The *Victoria County History* includes a general chapter or chapters on 'Architecture': there is also information in the parish accounts. Most space is devoted to military and ecclesiastical architecture. Periodical publications of local archaeological, architectural and historical societies often contain useful articles. So do national periodicals such as the archaeological publications listed on p. 72, architectural journals, and *Country Life* and *The Field*. Antiquaries' notes often describe buildings subsequently destroyed.

County and county borough *Development Plans* and planning surveys discuss local buildings. The local planning authority is empowered to list, and make preservation orders for, buildings of historical interest or special architectural merit, other than buildings on Ministry of Works lists and churches. The list is worth consulting, although the standard for inclusion varies and usually only brief descriptive details are given.

For architects, see J. Harvey, *English Medieval Architects* (Batsford, 1954) and H. M. Colvin, *A Biographical Dictionary of English Architects, 1660-1840* (Murray, 1954).

The following are also useful for quickly discovering important buildings of various kinds in a locality:

D. Knowles and R. N. Hadcock, *Medieval Religious Houses: England and Wales* (Longmans, 1953).

J. Betjeman ed., *Guide to English Parish Churches* (Collins, 1958).

H. M. Colvin ed., *The History of the King's Works, vols. i and ii, The Middle Ages* (H.M.S.O., 1963): 3 more vols. to be published.

Historic Houses, Castles and Gardens in Great Britain and Ireland (Index Publishers, annually).

C. Hussey and J. Cornforth, *English Country Houses Open to the Public* (4th ed., Country Life, 1964).

J. Lees Milne, *The National Trust Guide: Buildings* (Batsford, 1948): also National Trust *Atlas, List* and *Map* of properties and *Guides* to individual buildings.

Buildings

The Council for British Archaeology has published two useful short pamphlets, *The Recording of Architecture and its Publication* (Research Report, no. 2) and, more especially, *The Investigation of Smaller Domestic Buildings* (Research Report, no. 3). For record sources, see H. M. Colvin, 'Architectural History and its Records', *Archives*, vol. ii, no. 14 (1955), pp. 300-11.

ADDRESSES

LOCAL LIBRARIES, MUSEUMS AND SOCIETIES, AND LOCAL AUTHORITY DEPARTMENTS, such as architecture, engineering and planning, may have relevant material and knowledgeable members of staff.

For the Council for British Archaeology, the Ministry of Public Building and Works, and the Royal Commission on Historical Monuments (England), as well as some useful specialised societies, see pp. 72-73.

THE NATIONAL BUILDINGS RECORD, FIELDEN HOUSE, 10, GREAT COLLEGE STREET, LONDON, S.W.1. has the largest collection of photographs of buildings of historical interest.

THE MINISTRY OF HOUSING AND LOCAL GOVERNMENT (HISTORIC BUILDINGS DIVISION), WHITEHALL, LONDON, S.W.1. is concerned with the preservation of buildings of historical and architectural interest within the terms of planning acts.

THE SOCIETY FOR THE PROTECTION OF ANCIENT BUILDINGS, 55, GREAT ORMOND STREET, LONDON, W.C.1. publishes material relating to the history, care and repair of old buildings.

THE NATIONAL TRUST FOR PLACES OF HISTORIC INTEREST OR NATURAL BEAUTY, 42, QUEEN ANNE'S GATE, LONDON, S.W.1. is a private body acquiring land and houses for permanent preservation: for its publications, see p. 84.

Different types of building are the concern of societies such as:

THE HISTORIC CHURCHES PRESERVATION TRUST, FULHAM PALACE, LONDON, S.W.6.

THE ECCLESIOLOGICAL SOCIETY, c/o ST. ANNE'S VESTRY, CARTER LANE, LONDON, E.C.4.

THE NATIONAL ASSOCIATION OF ALMSHOUSES, BILLINGBEAR LODGE, WOKINGHAM, BERKS.

THE VERNACULAR ARCHITECTURE GROUP, 9, EAST COKER ROAD, YEOVIL, SOMERSET.

Buildings of different periods are the concern of societies such as:

THE GEORGIAN GROUP, 2, CHESTER STREET, LONDON, S.W.1.

THE VICTORIAN SOCIETY, 55, GREAT ORMOND STREET, LONDON, W.C.1.

THE LIBRARY OF THE SOCIETY OF GENEALOGISTS, 37, HARRINGTON GARDENS, LONDON, S.W.7., open to non-members on payment of a fee, is the best place for pursuing heraldic and genealogical matters, once local sources have been exhausted. There are various societies and journals devoted to the study of these subjects.

THE COLLEGE OF ARMS, QUEEN VICTORIA STREET, LONDON, E.C.3 is the authoritative body on heraldry.

Chapter 8 Archives

One of the main groups of written records available to the local historian, namely printed books and pamphlets, has already been described. Most of these are secondary authorities, but some, such as travellers' accounts, certain guidebooks and directories, constitute primary sources. The other major group of written material, archives, widely interpreted so as to include all historical manuscripts and documents, is described in this chapter. Once again, rigid divisions cannot be maintained. For example, while most archives represent primary source material, not all do; furthermore, since many records have been published, printed books are mentioned again here.

Documents are traditionally the historian's chief source of information and, despite what has been written earlier about the frequent and harmful neglect of other material and approaches, it cannot be denied that the written word remains the major, if not the sole, source from which knowledge of many aspects of local history can be derived. By definition, prehistory ends and history begins with the appearance of written records. These begin to be available for writing the history of this country from the time of the Roman occupation, and they thus span some two thousand years. A broad distinction can be drawn between the first and second parts of this period. Before approximately 1200 documents are not plentiful, and normally few are likely to be found which contain much detail about a particular place. For the years after 1200, however, England is fortunate in possessing a quantity and variety of material which is unparalleled elsewhere.

This material is sometimes divided into two categories, narrative accounts and records produced in the course of business of one kind or another. The former includes chronicles, histories, broadsheets and newspapers, the latter, documents produced by administrative, judicial and financial transactions. This division is not rigid; it may be difficult to decide in which category letters and diaries, for example, should be placed. Usually the local historian will find that the second group has more to offer him. However the material originated, the question of its authenticity may arise. It was formerly thought that narrative accounts, often written with an eye on posterity, were the more unreliable, but it should be noticed that the more technical records also need to be used critically. Most of them were not produced in order to answer the questions which historians usually ask of them, and consequently there is often the danger of misinterpretation.

Archives which may be useful to the local historian can be classified according to the bodies which produced them. The public central archives form the most important group: these comprise the records of central government from the eleventh to the twentieth century, as well as various collections of documents which have been acquired by the government at different times. The archives of local public bodies are represented by the records of the various units of local government, amongst which those of counties, cities and boroughs, and parishes are the most numerous and most important. Archives which can be described as semi-public include those of organisations such as public utility undertakings, endowed institutions and charitable trusts. Ecclesiastical archives embrace those of the Church of England and of the Roman Catholic and Nonconformist Churches. Their arrangement reflects church organisation so that there are, for example, Anglican collections at provincial, diocesan, archidiaconal and parochial level, besides the collections of Deans and Chapters of cathedrals. Records relating to the other churches are often more difficult to trace and to consult. Private archives are of many kinds. There are innumerable collections, large and small, of estate and family archives which vary enormously in the period and the area which they cover. Many business records fall into this category.

While provision has now been made for more than a

century for the records of the central government to be housed, catalogued and opened to public inspection, it is only in recent years that similar developments have taken place in respect of the majority of other archives. Since 1945, in particular, many repositories have been established and more documents have been made available for public use. The publicity which this movement has attracted, coupled with the increasing popularity, during the same period, of the study of local history, has produced large numbers of persons eager to use original records. Often they have little idea of the variety of records which exist or of how accessible or comprehensible they may be to them. In the following pages, therefore, an attempt is made to survey broadly the nature and location of records in order to help students and teachers to identify, more easily, relevant material suited to their needs.

PRINTED RECORDS

It is important to appreciate that a large amount of varied documentary material is readily accessible in print.

The contents of many, especially medieval documents, have been printed, either as texts or calendars. The former provide full transcriptions, with or without translations; the latter are summaries. There are two invaluable guides to this published material. R. Somerville, *Handlist of Record Publications* (British Records Association, 1951) arranges printed records by group and class document. E. L. C. Mullins, *Texts and Calendars* (Royal Historical Society, 1958) reverses the process by listing publications under the societies which produced them. These societies include official bodies such as the Public Record Office and the Royal Commission on Historical Monuments, and a variety of national societies like the Harleian Society, specialising in heraldic and genealogical material, the Navy Records Society, and the Selden Society which publishes legal records, as well as county, area and borough organisations. All students who are interested in archives relating to their neighbourhood should consult these two guides. Published documents will also often be found in local histories and in other books and articles. Besides the material just described, which has been published by historians, many modern records, printed by the organisation which produced them, are available. Council minutes and the reports of various officials are good examples of such useful, and often neglected, printed sources.

HINTS FOR THOSE CONSIDERING WORK ON ORIGINAL DOCUMENTS

Anyone who intends to work on original documents must realise that he is likely to encounter a variety of problems and be prepared to help himself to overcome them. He will need to know the chief record offices and broadly what they contain. He will soon realise that a large proportion of the material concerning a locality will not be near at hand. Many records will also be written in a strange language. Before 1066, this is Latin or Old English; after the Conquest it is usually Latin, but sometimes Norman-French. Although English was used increasingly from the sixteenth century, Latin remained the language of most courts until as recently as 1731. While medieval Latin is simpler in form than its classical counterpart, it obviously constitutes an obstacle in the study of many documents. Styles of handwriting, too, will be unfamiliar at first. Text or book hand was employed throughout the Middle Ages for documents of lasting importance, while various forms of court hand were used from the thirteenth century onwards for less formal purposes. After 1500 secretary hand and its derivatives produce, for a century or so, some of the most difficult documents to decipher. From about 1700, most handwriting is usually no more difficult to read than that of the present day. Abbreviations were often used, and these have to be learned. Some knowledge of chronology is necessary in order to understand, for example, the dating of documents, and seals may have to be identified and interpreted.

There are several standard guides and handbooks to help the student tackle the difficulties which have been mentioned, and instruction in reading documents may be available in evening classes or week-end schools organised by the W.E.A. or the University Extra-Mural Department. F. G. Emmison, *Archives and Local History* (Methuen, 1966), which deals with post-medieval local records, is the best introduction to the use of local archives. See also L. J. Redstone and F. W. Steer eds., *Local Records: their Nature and Care* (Bell, 1953).

A good idea of the main classes of record which are of use to the student of local history can be obtained by studying F. G. Emmison, *Archives and Local History* (Methuen, 1966); W. O. Hassall, *Wheatley Records, 956-1956* (Oxfordshire Record Society, 1956); P. A. Kennedy ed., *Nottinghamshire Historical Documents in Facsimile* (Nottingham, Local History Council, 1962); and J. West, *Village Records* (Macmillan, 1962). There is a useful series, 'Short Guides to Records' in *History* (1962-). The books by Emmison, Kennedy and West include facsimiles, with transcriptions and translations where necessary, of many documents, and so form good introductions to Latin and palaeography as well as to record types. H. E. P. Grieve, *Examples of English Handwriting, 1150-1750* (2nd ed., Chelmsford, Essex County Council, 1959) is useful for the same purpose and refers to more advanced works on the subject. E. A. Gooder, *Latin for Local History* (Longmans, 1961) is an introductory manual. R. E. Latham comp., *Revised Medieval Latin Word List* (Oxford University Press, 1965) is the best dictionary, and C. T. Martin, *The Record Interpreter* (2nd ed., Stevens, 1910) contains several useful lists of, for example, abbreviations, names, and Norman-French words. For regnal years, saints' days, and problems of chronology generally, see F. M. Powicke and E. B. Fryde, *Handbook of British Chronology* (2nd ed., Royal Historical Society, 1961) and C. R. Cheney, *Handbook of Dates for Students of English History* (Rev. ed., Royal Historical Society, 1961). Seals are described in H. S. Kingsford, *Seals* (Helps for Students of History, 1920): both the Public Record Office and British Museum have large collections of seals to which there are published guides.

Before particular classes of records are consulted, the problems which they may pose should be considered and only manageable tasks should be undertaken. The student will need to be familiar with the general background to the topic on which he is working and the administrative organisation which produced the records which he intends to study. Documents later than 1700 present great, and neglected, opportunities for study and few problems of language and handwriting. Some rewarding topics in this period which are normally well-documented are listed in R. Douch and F. W. Steer, *Local History Essays: Some Notes for Students* (University of Southampton, 1960) which also provides other help for the beginner. Even if the enquirer hopes to study earlier records, it is often a good plan to begin with recent, intelligible documents which deal with a recognisable society and problems, and to work backwards from these. Before any class of original documents is studied, it is wise to find out as much as possible about its scope, form and vocabulary by consulting a book on records and, where necessary, referring to a printed transcription or summary of such documents. Half the battle in reading records lies in knowing what to expect. If there is a printed guide to the contents of the repository which is to be visited, this should, of course, be carefully consulted. The availability of other aids will vary from office to office, but enquiries should always be made as to the existence of brief catalogues or more detailed calendars of different classes of records, and of indexes of parishes, persons, and/or subjects. Only reasonable requests for assistance and for the production of documents should be made. Where it is difficult to consult the originals, or where copies are needed for some purpose, it is usually possible to arrange for photocopies of documents to be supplied. If documents have to be transcribed, *Notes for the Guidance of Editors of Record Publications* (British Records Association, 1946) may be helpful.

RECORD REPOSITORIES

The broad groups of archives described above are to be found in a variety of repositories and in private hands. A particular repository often houses archives from more than one group. Some record offices, if only because of their accessibility, are likely to attract more students of local history than others, and the order in which the main collections are described here has been adopted for this reason. A list, compiled by the Historical Manuscripts Commission and the British Records Association, of *Record Repositories in Great Britain* (H.M.S.O., 1964) gives addresses, hours of opening, general contents and facilities. Students using records for historical, as distinct from legal, purposes are admitted to most repositories free of charge. Not all private collections, of course, are open to inspection.

The Parish Chest

Parish records relate to both ecclesiastical and civil affairs. Many ecclesiastical parishes were established before the Norman Conquest and, from the later Middle Ages to the nineteenth century, their officers had the execution of varied civil business entrusted to them. In 1894, civil parishes were created, the records of which should be in the custody of the Clerk to the Parish Council. The student might expect, therefore, that the records in the chest or safe of an old-established Anglican church would illustrate ecclesiastical history from the Middle Ages to the present and civil affairs from the sixteenth century to 1894: in practice, ecclesiastical records earlier than 1500 are rare. The chief classes of ecclesiastical material are the registers of baptisms, marriages and burials; churchwardens' accounts; tithe and glebe records; and miscellaneous items relating to the fabric and furniture of the church. Civil records consist chiefly of vestry minutes which cover many aspects of local life, the accounts of officials, especially the constable and the surveyor of the highways, and, often most voluminous of all, an assortment of records concerning poverty and poor relief from the early seventeenth to the early nineteenth century.

W. E. Tate, *The Parish Chest* (3rd ed., Cambridge University Press, 1960) discusses the evolution of the parish, its officers and documents. Catalogues of parish records have been issued for some counties, Essex and Shropshire, for example. K. Blomfield and H. K. Percy-Smith, *National Index of Parish Register Copies* (Society of Genealogists, 1939) is now under revision. In many counties, to ensure safe custody, parish records are being deposited in the County Record Office.

The County Record Office

All English counties, except Rutland, now have an official County Record Office, staffed by professional archivists. Apart from a few counties, such as Bedfordshire and Essex, these have been established since 1945. While these repositories contain both medieval and modern records, they usually have more of the latter.

County records, the records of county administration, are housed in them. These include a variety of material, often from the sixteenth century onwards, relating to the manifold judicial and administrative duties of the Courts of Quarter Sessions. Crimes and offences, jury service, rates, roads, bridges, gaols, poor relief, ale houses, trade, fairs and markets, hospitals and asylums, and Nonconformity and Roman Catholicism are among the subjects which figure in these records, often with a wealth of human detail. Documents deposited by law, so that they could be consulted by interested local parties, are also found, embracing topics such as charities and friendly societies, parliamentary elections, taxation, enclosures, canals, turnpikes, railways, and early public utilities. There may also be records of Petty Sessions, and material arising from the work of the Lord Lieutenant, the Sheriff, and the Coroner. An ever-increasing quantity of archives relates to the work of the County Council, since its creation in 1888, and its various committees: much of this, however, may not be open to public inspection without special permission. There are also the records of bodies which have been taken over by County Councils, such as Highway Boards, School Boards, and Boards of Guardians.

Other kinds of records, which are described in detail later, are increasingly being deposited in County Record Offices. Thus estate and family archives occur in varying numbers in all; diocesan and archidiaconal records are being transferred to them; and, in many areas, parish records are being deposited.

F. G. Emmison and I. Gray, *County Records* (Rev. ed., Historical Association, 1961) is a useful introduction. Since most offices are fairly recent establishments, some have been so busy ensuring the safe custody of records that they have not yet produced many aids to consulting them. Many offices, however, have printed guides to their collections. If there is not one available for the county in which the student is interested, consultation of any good guide, for example that for the Essex, Kent or Lancashire office, will indicate the types of documents which are likely to be found. The local archivist's *Annual Reports* may be helpful. Unpublished catalogues and/or indexes may have been compiled. Some county records have been printed, especially Quarter Sessions records: the pamphlet by Emmison and Gray contains a list of these.

The Borough Record Office

The situation in boroughs varies. Some, especially of the large, ancient cities and boroughs, have an archives department in the municipal offices, in the care perhaps of a qualified archivist. Elsewhere, the local library or more rarely the museum, houses the record collection: see P. Hepworth, *Archives and Manuscripts in Libraries* (2nd ed., Library Association, 1964). The records of small boroughs are often deposited in the County Record Office. Some borough collections include both local public archives and other classes; some have only one or the other.

Public borough archives, the amount and variety of which are likely to depend on the antiquity, status and size of particular boroughs, are concerned with municipal administrative, legal, financial and commercial matters. They usually include medieval material, as in Bristol and Southampton, for example, and many go back to the sixteenth century. Such records contain information relating to the borough's income and expenditure, property, courts, trade, and customs and privileges; municipal and parliamentary elections; and gilds and charities. Records of Improvement Commissioners are often found for the eighteenth and early nineteenth centuries, and there will also be the more recent records of the present local government authority. F. J. C. Hearnshaw, *Municipal Records* (S.P.C.K., 1918) and Redstone and Steer, *Local Records*, chapter XVIII, briefly survey borough records. Few detailed guides or catalogues have been published, but many lists have been issued by the Historical Manuscripts Commission (see p. 98) and individual records, especially medieval documents, have been printed by local societies.

The Diocesan Record Office

Diocesan records include bishops' registers, administrative records, records of ecclesiastical courts, and visitation documents. Amongst important topics covered are ordinations and institutions to benefices; tithe and glebe; the church fabric; the licensing of Dissenters' meeting houses; baptisms, marriages and burials; and the behaviour of the clergy and laity. There may also be estate documents similar to those produced in the administration of lay estates, though many of these have been transferred to the offices of the Church Commissioners, Millbank, London, S.W.1.

For diocesan records in particular areas, see L. M. Midgley and P. M. Ward, 'Survey of the Principal Collections of the Archives of the Church of England' (Pilgrim Trust, TS., 1952). Until recently these records were usually in the custody of diocesan registrars, and were often difficult of access. Many collections have now been deposited in county record offices. So have most archidiaconal records, which deal with many of the same topics. The archiepiscopal records of Canterbury are at Lambeth Palace, London, and of York at The Borthwick Institute of Historical Research in that city.

Not much diocesan material has been printed, but see the bishops' registers published by local bodies and by the Canterbury and York Society, and two books by J. S. Purvis, *Introduction to Ecclesiastical Records* (York, St. Anthony's Press, 1963) and *Tudor Parish Documents in the Diocese of York* (Cambridge University Press, 1948). E. R. C. Brinkworth has three valuable articles on 'Evidence from Ecclesiastical Sources' in *The Amateur Historian*, vol. ii, nos. 1-3 (1954-55), and there are others by D. M. Owen, 'The Use of Ecclesiastical

Records for Secular Subjects' and 'How to Study your Parish Church from Documents' in the same journal, vol. v., no. 2 (1962) and vol. vii, no. 1 (1966). See also E. R. C. Brinkworth, 'The Study and Use of Archdeacons' Court Records', *Transactions of the Royal Historical Society*, 4th Series, vol. xxv (1943).

The District Probate Registry

Testamentary matters were almost entirely the concern of ecclesiastical courts until 1857. Civil District Probate Registries were then established from which documents, dated usually from the fourteenth century to 1857, have recently been transferred to county record offices. Wills and inventories are the main and most useful classes of such records. Those of people with property in more than one county will normally be found, not in the local office, but among the records of the Prerogative Court of Canterbury which are now in the Principal Probate Registry at Somerset House. Many post-1858 wills have likewise been transferred from District Probate Registries to local record offices: they can also be consulted at Somerset House. A. J. Camp, *Wills and their Whereabouts* (Canterbury, Phillimore, 1963) is the indispensable guide to all aspects of this subject.

The value of wills in genealogical studies has long been realised, and various indexes, listed in Camp's book, have been published. In the last few years, social and economic historians have begun to use the inventories which often accompany wills: see four articles, 'Inventories as a Source of Local History' in *The Amateur Historian*, vol. iv, nos. 4, 5 and 6 (1959-60).

Business Archives

Interest in business archives developed late and fewer survive than might be expected. The histories of some large industries have been written recently, and some ledgers, correspondence files and papers have been deposited in local record offices. The collections of solicitors and auctioneers and estate agents are particularly valuable because they illustrate, not only the development of a particular firm, but also other aspects of local history. See T. C. Barker *et al.*, *Business History* (Historical Association, 1960). The Business Archives Council, 63, Queen Victoria Street, London, E.C.4., has a library of published histories, research collections, and lists of records: it also publishes *Business Archives.*

Private Collections

Private archives vary enormously in size and scope from the one or two records, which most people possess, to vast collections of estate, household and personal documents. The latter may include a great variety of material, such as deeds of title, leases, indentures, agreements, estate surveys, rentals, maps, manorial court records, accounts, diaries, wills, letters, and commercial correspondence. Where members of a family have been prominent in local or national affairs, private muniments may also contain public records produced in the course of official duties.

Since 1869 the Historical Manuscripts Commission, Quality Court, Chancery Lane, London, W.C.2. has been surveying many of the large, private collections held, for example, by families, religious foundations, colleges, schools and almshouses. Sectional List no. 17, *Publications of the Royal Commission on Historical Manuscripts,* (H.M.S.O.) lists its detailed calendars and other publications. There is a *Guide to the Reports of the Royal Commission on Historical Manuscripts, 1870-1911, Part I, Index of Places* (1914) and *Part II, Index of Persons* (1935-38): a volume bringing these up to 1957 is to be published shortly. There is an 'Index to all the Collections reported on up to 1942' in the *22nd Report,* pp. 66-103. 'A General Analytical Survey and Key' is also in preparation which will serve as a guide and index of subjects.

In 1945 the National Register of Archives was established as part of the Historical Manuscripts Commission. Its original task was to record the location, content and availability of all collections of documents in England and Wales, excluding central government records. It has now also become an important centre of information. Voluntary local workers send in lists of documents to headquarters, which publishes a *List of Accessions to Repositories* (H.M.S.O.) annually and a *Bulletin* periodically. Indexes to the owners and location of documents, and of their contents under persons, subjects and places, are kept, and these can be consulted by appointment.

Many private documents are deposited in county and borough record offices and in national and public libraries. Indeed, national repositories contain many documents of local interest: unfortunately their relative inaccessibility may prevent many students from using them.

The Public Record Office, Chancery Lane, London, W.C.2.

This repository, as already seen, contains the records of the central government, medieval and modern. M. S. Giuseppi, *Guide to the Contents of the Public Record Office*, 2 vols. (Rev. ed., H.M.S.O., 1963) indicates the vast quantity, arrangement and scope of the documents deposited there. V. H. Galbraith, *An Introduction to the Use of the Public Records* (Oxford University Press, 1934) is a useful introduction. M. S. Giuseppi, *Guide to Archives relating to Surrey in the Public Record Office* (Surrey Record Society, 1925) shows the classes of records which can be expected to yield the fullest information for any county. Not all series are complete, however. Many classes are arranged by counties. A valuable series of *Lists and Indexes* has been published and there are additional manuscript indexes in the office.

A great deal of material has been printed by the government, sometimes in full, but more usually in calendar form. Full details are given in *Government Publications, Sectional List 24, Printed Records,* often known as *List* Q and obtainable free of charge, from H.M.S.O., 49 High Holborn, London, W.C.1. Most volumes are well indexed and are a mine of information. Giuseppi, *Guide* indicates the kind of information which each class of record contains. Among the Chancery records, *Charter Rolls, Patent Rolls, Close Rolls, Fine Rolls,* and *Inquisitions* are in print for long periods in the Middle Ages. Of Exchequer archives, see especially *Domesday Book,* the *Book of Fees*, and *Feudal Aids* which contain much information on feudal tenures: cf. H. Hall ed., *The Red Book of the Exchequer*, 3 vols. (Rolls Series, 1896) and *Ancient Deeds*. Few legal records have been printed: but see *Curia Regis Rolls* and *Placita de Quo Warranto*. Other medieval records have been published by societies or individuals: these include classes such as Pipe Rolls, the accounts of the medieval sheriff rendered at the Exchequer; Feet of Fines which contain topographical and genealogical information in connection with land conveyance; and Inquisitions post mortem, surveys of land made at the death of tenants-in-chief.

Published modern records date mainly from the period c.1500-c.1775. See especially *Letters and Papers, Henry VIII*; *State Papers Domestic*; *State Papers, Foreign*; *Acts of the Privy Council*; and *Treasury Papers and Books*. Again, see *Sectional List 24* and Giuseppi's *Guide* for full details. Some classes of modern records have been published locally for many counties; for example, lists of church goods and chantry certificates made in the reign of Edward VI.

Manuscript transcriptions of some public records, made by local antiquaries, will often be found in local libraries and museums.

There are commentaries on, or guides to, many particular classes of records. It is impossible to list many of these, but the beginner may find the following especially valuable: two series of articles in *The Amateur Historian*, vol. i, nos. 1-6 (1952-53) and vol. vi, no. 6—(1965-); R. Welldon Finn, *An Introduction to Domesday Book* (Longmans, 1963); A. Ballard, J. Tait and M. Weinbaum, *British Borough Charters, 1042-1660*, 3 vols. (Cambridge University Press, 1913-43); M. W. Beresford, *The Lay Subsidies and Poll Taxes of 1377, 1379 and 1381* (Canterbury, Phillimore, 1963); *Census Reports of Great Britain, 1801-1931* (H.M.S.O., 1951); and M. W. Beresford, *The Unprinted Census Returns of 1841, 1851, 1861 for England and Wales* (Canterbury, Phillimore, 1966).

The House of Lords Record Office, London, S.W.1.

This office contains the voluminous records of parliament

since 1497, earlier parliamentary records being in the Public Record Office. While they concern the work of both Lords and Commons, not many Commons' papers survived the fire of 1834.

M. Bond, *The Records of Parliament: a Guide for Genealogists and Local Historians* (Canterbury, Phillimore, 1964) describes the nature and value of, and aids to, using Acts of Parliament, Private Bill Records, Parliamentary Papers and Judicial Records, and Parliamentary Debates. For Parliamentary Papers, see also W. R. Powell, *Local History from Blue Books: a Select List of the Sessional Papers of the House of Commons* (Historical Association, 1962). These records are a rich, and greatly neglected, source of local information.

Several *Calendars of the Manuscripts of the House of Lords* have been published. Copies of some of the printed material, such as Bills, Acts and Parliamentary Papers, are sometimes available in local libraries.

The British Museum, Bloomsbury, London, W.C.1.

The Department of Manuscripts has been built up piecemeal by gift, bequest and purchase. Unlike the records in the Public Record Office, therefore, this collection does not represent the product of an administrative system, and it is correspondingly more difficult to know in advance what it may contain and to search in it. For a short survey of the great variety of documentary material, see J. P. Gilson, *A Student's Guide to the Manuscripts of the British Museum* (S.P.C.K., 1920).

No series of published records is issued, but many documents have been printed by societies and individuals. Printed catalogues are available: see T. C. Skeat, *The Catalogues of the Manuscript Collections in the British Museum* (Rev. ed., The Museum, 1962).

University Libraries and Private Libraries

These, *e.g.* the John Rylands Library at Manchester and Dr. Williams' Library, 14, Gordon Square, London, W.C.1, have collections which are similar in character to that of the British Museum. Printed aids to using them may be available.

SPECIAL TOPICS

On many occasions the student will wish to know the chief documentary sources for specific topics of local interest. These will vary from individual to individual and from place to place, and so it is impossible to consider them in detail here. R. B. Pugh, *How to Write a Parish History* (Allen and Unwin, 1954); W. G. Hoskins, *Local History in England* (Longmans, 1959); and F. Celoria, *Teach Yourself Local History* (English Universities Press, 1959) are all arranged on such a basis: they cover topics such as the manor, the parish, the town, the old community, agriculture, communications, the church, non-conformity, charities, schools, population, and family history.

The following is a short list of books and articles which would help in the launching of work on a few popular subjects:

M. Gelling, 'Pre-Conquest Local History from Anglo-Saxon Charters', *The Amateur Historian*, vol. i, no. 8 (1953).

G. R. C. Davis, *Medieval Cartularies of Great Britain* (Longmans, 1958).

N. J. Hone, *The Manor and Manorial Records* (3rd ed. Methuen, 1925).

C. J. Cornwall, *How to Read Old Title Deeds* (University of Birmingham, 1964).

R. H. Hilton, 'The Content and Sources of English Agrarian History before 1500', and J. Thirsk, '. . . after 1500', *Agricultural History Review*, vol. iii (1955).

W. R. Powell, 'The Sources for the History of Protestant Nonconformist Churches in England', *Bulletin of the Institute of Historical Research*, vol. xxv, no. 72 (1952). Most churches have their own historical society and journal.

W. K. Jordan, *The Charities of Rural England, 1480-1660* (Allen and Unwin, 1961).

J. S. Purvis, *Educational Records* (York, St. Anthony's Press, 1959).

S. and B. Webb, *English Local Government*, 9 vols. (Longmans, 1906-29).

Archives

J. Simmons, 'Railway History in English Local Records', *Journal of Transport History*, vol. i, no. 3 (1954).

L. C. Johnson, 'Records of the British Transport Commission', *The Amateur Historian*, vol. iv, no. 8 (1960).

H. J. Dyos, *Victorian Suburb* (Leicester University Press, 1961). J. Thirsk, *Sources of Information on Population, 1500-1760, and Unexpected Sources in Local Records* (Canterbury, Phillimore, 1965) and E. A. Wrigley ed., *An Introduction to English Historical Demography* (Weidenfeld and Nicolson, 1966).

J. Taylor, *The Use of Medieval Chronicles* (Historical Association, 1965).

W. Matthews, *British Diaries* (University of California Press, 1950) and *British Autobiographies* (University of California Press, 1955).

See also articles in periodicals such as *The Amateur Historian, Archives* and the journals of specialist societies.

Chapter 9 Pictorial Records

There are various pictorial records which are often useful to the local historian. Only very rarely will illuminations in medieval manuscripts throw light on the history of a particular locality, and the earliest relevant material may well consist of maps (see pp. 35-38).

PAINTINGS, DRAWINGS, ETCHINGS AND ENGRAVINGS

Paintings, drawings, etchings and engravings, especially of subjects such as people, topographical scenes, and buildings and details from them, are commonly found. While some may have originated in any century from the sixteenth to the twentieth, most will usually date from about 1700-1900. Some will be in books: many more will probably have been produced, or will now be kept, separately. Sometimes isolated illustrations will be discovered; but there are also important collections to be searched which often include material gathered, or produced, by local antiquaries.

Some pictorial records possess artistic merit: here we are concerned only with their value as historical sources. Paintings, drawings, etchings and engravings can supply information which cannot be obtained in any other way. Their testimony should not, however, be accepted uncritically, and should be checked, wherever possible. Expert advice may be needed. Is the family portrait an original? Who painted it? Does it represent the person traditionally associated with it? Is it a likeness? How far are the scenes of town and countryside impressionistic? And exactly when, and by whom, were they painted or drawn? Assigning a date and identifying the artist are always important, and often difficult, tasks.

PHOTOGRAPHS

Photographs are likely to provide the largest quantity of pictorial records in most local investigations. The danger of personal interpretation and misrepresentation by the artist is obviously less with photographs than it is with the other types of illustrations just described: nevertheless, it must not be forgotten that the camera can and does, sometimes lie. Various useful groups of photographs can be distinguished. Again, while some of these form part of established collections, others will be encountered in a variety of places as the investigation proceeds. A valuable service will be performed in ensuring the safe custody of the latter, since many are in constant danger of destruction.

Picture postcards are valuable, especially for the late Victorian and Edwardian periods, between the invention of photography and the widespread use of individually-owned cameras. These cards commonly depict street scenes; individual buildings, such as churches, inns, shops and workshops, and they frequently include details of, for example, contemporary costume and transport facilities. Many also commemorate important local occasions, festivities, processions and family ceremonies, or groups like local teams and children at school. During this century the function of the local photographer in producing this second kind of record has been increasingly taken over by the press photographer, and newspaper photographs constitute another important group. The quality of these, especially the older ones, is not always good.

There are many collections of photographs relating to particular aspects of local history with which the student may be concerned. Some of these are housed locally, others are in national repositories. Geology, archaeological sites, buildings, and architectural detail are amongst the main subjects covered. A list of some of the most useful collections, most of which are arranged on a topographical basis, is given later.

AERIAL PHOTOGRAPHS

One type of modern photograph, the value of which is not

always appreciated, is the aerial photograph. For some archaeological and historical purposes vertical photographs are useful, for others oblique views reveal more. For a settlement as a whole the air photograph supplies a bird's eye view which is seldom obtainable from any natural or man-made vantage point. It not only contains a mass of detail, but also enables general characteristics and relationships to be more readily observed. A view of a more restricted area may yield additional information about a particular site which is visible on the ground. Thus, the position and plan of a castle or monastery may be strikingly illuminated. Even more impressive, archaeological sites which are scarcely visible or completely unknown by observation at ground level are frequently delineated in aerial photographs. These are revealed as variations in the black and white photograph produced by soil and crop coloration and by shadows cast by earthworks or crops of varying height. Once soil has been disturbed, it holds more moisture: greener and taller crops result. Where the foundations of buildings lie just beneath the surface, growth is poor. Even quite slight earthworks, depressions as well as mounds, cast significant shadows, especially in oblique photographs taken when the sun is low. The presence of features such as burial mounds, field systems, villa sites, and lost villages is often betrayed by clues of this kind. The interpretation of aerial photographs is not always easy, and there are many details which can mislead the beginner. Stereoscopic pairs are a useful aid.

BOOKS

Useful general works include N. Pevsner, *The Englishness of English Art* (Architectural Press, 1956); L. Binyon, *English Water Colours* (2nd ed., Black, 1944); C. Hussey, *British Country Life in Art* (Country Life, 1937); J. R. Abbey, *Life in England in Aquatint and Lithography, 1770-1860* (Curwen Press, 1953); J. R. Abbey, *Scenery of Great Britain and Ireland in Aquatint and Lithography, 1770-1860* (Curwen Press, 1952); and A. G. Reynolds, *Painters of the Victorian Scene* (Batsford, 1953). See also the Oxford *History of English Art* and the Pelican *History of Art* series, and their bibliographies.

J. K. St. Joseph, ed., *The Uses of Air Photography* (John Baker, 1966) contains articles in which specialists discuss the value of air photography in the study of subjects like archaeology, geography, and history. For particular kinds of sites, see O. G. S. Crawford and A. Keiller, *Wessex from the Air* (Oxford University Press, 1928), which is particularly concerned with prehistoric remains on chalk downs; M. W. Beresford and J. K. St. Joseph, *Medieval England: an Aerial Survey* (Cambridge University Press, 1958); W. D. Simpson, *Castles from the Air* (Country Life, 1949); and D. Knowles and J. K. St. Joseph, *Monastic Sites from the Air* (Cambridge University Press, 1952).

For those interested in taking photographs, the Library Association has in preparation a book on historical record photography. Meanwhile, H. D. Gower, L. S. Jast and W. W. Topley, *The Camera as Historian* (Sampson, Low, 1916), though out of date in some respects, is still useful. See also M. B. Cookson, *Photography for Archaeologists* (Parrish, 1954). In some localities camera clubs or photographic societies make surveys of archaeological, architectural and historical subjects: Manchester, Northamptonshire and Worcestershire, for example, are active in this respect.

There are now several methods of copying documents cheaply: see O. Croy, *Camera Copying and Reproduction* (Focal Press, 1964). *The Visual Education Year Book* (1963) has a valuable list of 'Material for Making Non-Projected Aids'.

ADDRESSES

LOCAL COLLECTIONS. Pictorial records are usually held by public libraries and museums and, on a smaller scale, by record offices. Local authority engineers, architects and planners often have photographs. Society libraries and individuals are likely to have material. Old established local photographers, postcard publishers, and shops selling cards may have old, and historically valuable, stock. Newspaper offices frequently have negatives and prints as well as back numbers of their newspapers. Aerial photographs of local sites are often held by museums and planning departments.

Some local collections contain material concerning several counties: the 'Dryden Collection' in Northampton Public Library (*Catalogue*, 1912) is one which includes notes and drawings for most counties.

THE BRITISH MUSEUM, BLOOMSBURY, LONDON, W.C.1. has a special Department of Prints and Drawings. The Department of Manuscripts also includes maps, plans and topographical drawings.

THE BODLEIAN LIBRARY, OXFORD. See especially, but not solely, the 'Gough Collection' of topographical prints and engravings of the British Isles.

THE NATIONAL PORTRAIT GALLERY, ST. MARTIN'S PLACE, LONDON, W.C.2. has started to compile a national record of family portraits: information can be obtained from the Director. See also W. G. Constable, *Collections of Historical Portraits and Other Forms of Iconography in Great Britain* (Historical Association, 1934), and the other national galleries.

THE GEOLOGICAL SURVEY AND MUSEUM, EXHIBITION ROAD, SOUTH KENSINGTON, LONDON, S.W.7. issues a catalogue of *Classified Geological Photographs* (3rd ed., H.M.S.O., 1963) from its collections. See also the lists published by the Geological Photographs Committee of the British Association, Burlington House, Piccadilly, London, W.1.

THE MUSEUM OF ENGLISH RURAL LIFE, WHITEKNIGHTS PARK, UNIVERSITY OF READING, has a large collection relating to farm tools and implements.

THE NATIONAL MARITIME MUSEUM, GREENWICH, LONDON, S.E.10: for shipping and ports.

THE SCIENCE MUSEUM, SOUTH KENSINGTON, LONDON, S.W.7: for developments in applied science; for example, transport, industry, engineering.

THE VICTORIA AND ALBERT MUSEUM, SOUTH KENSINGTON, LONDON, S.W.7: for fine and applied art; for example, architecture, ceramics, metalwork, textiles, woodwork, costume.

THE MINISTRY OF PUBLIC BUILDING AND WORKS, LAMBETH BRIDGE HOUSE, ALBERT EMBANKMENT, LONDON, S.E.1 has a national collection relating especially to archaeological sites and buildings.

THE ROYAL COMMISSION ON HISTORICAL MONUMENTS (ENGLAND),

FIELDEN HOUSE, GREAT COLLEGE STREET, LONDON, S.W.I. also has a large collection concerning archaeological sites and buildings.

THE NATIONAL BUILDINGS RECORD, FIELDEN HOUSE, GREAT COLLEGE STREET, LONDON, S.W.I. has the largest collection of architectural photographs of England and Wales.

THE CENTRAL COUNCIL FOR THE CARE OF CHURCHES, 83, LONDON WALL, LONDON, E.C.2: for churches and their contents. Prints are not normally supplied.

THE CURATOR OF THE INSTITUTE OF AERIAL PHOTOGRAPHY, SELWYN COLLEGE, CAMBRIDGE, is the custodian of the best national collection of air photographs taken for archaeological and historical purposes. There is no published index, and enquiry should be made by letter.

THE ASHMOLEAN MUSEUM, OXFORD, THE BRITISH MUSEUM, BLOOMSBURY, LONDON, W.C.I., and THE ORDNANCE SURVEY, MAYBUSH, SOUTHAMPTON, all have collections. The Ministry of Defence has a vast stock of aerial photographs. For various reasons, not all are technically suitable for present purposes and others are not available because of security restrictions. Applications to purchase should be submitted through the local branch of the Ministry of Housing and Local Government.

AEROFILMS AND AERO PICTORIAL LTD., 4, ALBEMARLE STREET, LONDON, W.I. is the most useful to the local historian of private firms which supply aerial photographs not all of which are taken primarily for archaeological or historical purposes: see their *Classified Index to the Library of Aerial Photographs* (Rev. ed., 1962).

All the above collections can be consulted and arrangements can usually be made for copies to be supplied.

Photographs can also be obtained from many of the specialised societies and repositories mentioned in earlier chapters. See, too, G. W. A. Nunn ed., *British Sources of Photographs and Pictures* (Cassell, 1952) which lists both national and local repositories and commercial collections and photographers, and E. J. Priestley, 'Illustrating Local History', *The Amateur Historian*, vol. vii, no. 2 (1966).

Chapter 10 People

People are a useful source of information in many local history studies: in some, they are indispensable. Such helpers may be officials, usually public servants, part of whose work it is to assist students of local history. Or they may be officers of various departments and organisations, both public and private, or private individuals who would not normally expect to answer enquiries of an historical nature from members of the public, but who may be approached because they have specialised knowledge or are the custodians of relevant material.

HELPFUL PEOPLE

The addresses of many people who may be able and willing to help in a variety of studies have been included in earlier chapters and will not be repeated. Most of these are librarians, archivists, curators, secretaries of learned societies, and departmental officials, who are likely to possess specialised knowledge relating to particular aspects of local history. A few private persons have also been mentioned, but it is necessary here to consider in more detail the contribution which local inhabitants may be able to offer in local studies.

Many communities have their unofficial local historian or historians to whom enquiries tend to be passed. Their qualifications and ability vary considerably, but nearly all are storehouses of detailed, if often unrelated, local information, and many are much more than that. Some members of local historical and archaeological societies are experts in their fields. Rural communities in particular, but not solely, are also likely to have other people who are generally knowledgeable, especially about the present and the recent past. These often include the rector or vicar, the schoolteacher, the postmaster or postmistress, and the publican.

People

Most of the people mentioned so far are in the nature of secondary sources: they have knowledge about sources of information or about aspects of local history which they have acquired and which they may be willing to pass on. There are others who constitute primary sources, handing on the stuff of history itself, either by their actions or by word of mouth. Old inhabitants will often be the most useful in this category. Memories of the changes witnessed in the neighbourhood during the lifetime of an eighty- or ninety-year-old inhabitant are well worth recording in any generation. At present they are especially valuable since today's old people have experienced the transformation of local life brought about by mechanisation and by improved means of transport and communication. Their lives bridge two very different worlds, and their reminiscences need to be obtained quickly if they are not to be lost for ever.

Besides their memories of events which have happened during their lifetime, old people, and sometimes younger ones, may also be able to demonstrate long-established crafts or practices, or be valuable repositories of traditional information on many subjects. Craftsmen at work, such as thatchers, hurdlemakers and charcoal burners, as well as the representatives of more localised old pursuits, may reveal the habits of centuries in their dress, equipment, language or posture. Local customs connected with special occasions or particular dates can also be illuminating. Thus baptisms, marriages and burials are celebrated in various ways, while the Christmas mummers, Shrove Tuesday pancake-tossing, and the corn dollies and supper of harvest time are common examples of calendar customs. A variety of superstitions and beliefs may be remembered and, perhaps, still practised. In some areas, for example, a solitary crow flying over the house is an ominous sign, while to have two magpies cross one's path denotes good fortune. A belief, more widespread than might be imagined, in witchcraft is sometimes encountered. Old recipes and remedies are likely to be recalled or be still in use: for instance, various instructions for making wine and curing warts are frequently heard. Children's games and rhymes, folk songs and dances, and proverbs, legends and stories represent yet other kinds of lore which can often be supplied by local people. Stories of goblins and fairies are associated with many local sites of archaeological interest. Whatever may be the content of the traditional knowledge which local inhabitants are able to impart, such information will usually be given orally to the investigator; further valuable historical material, in the form of local words and dialect, will thus be made available.

Some old people will, if asked, write down their memories. With others, notes can be made by the student during conversation. Often the best method is to record informal interviews on tape, the actual speech of the informant thus being preserved as well as his information. Collecting oral traditions and memories is not usually as straightforward as it may seem, and the procedure to be followed with a particular person may well depend on his personality and attitude. Questions need to be carefully devised and interviews cannot be hurried. Many old people enjoy talking, but are easily upset or diverted from one topic to another. Often the same items will be repeated many times.

Finally, it is important that oral evidence, from whatever source it is derived, should, if possible, always be checked. Memories are often unreliable, leg-pulling is not unknown, and oral traditions are by no means invariably well-founded in fact. Drains masquerading as underground passages, and parish churches or private dwellings alleged to have been medieval religious houses are very common examples of the latter.

ASKING FOR HELP

It is unfortunate that in recent years the kindness of many people, both public officials and private persons, has been abused by a large number of enquirers into local history. It would be easy to quote specific examples of students of all ages who have expected librarians to provide references which they could have easily collected for themselves, who have regarded archivists almost as their research assistants, or who have called on private individuals, unannounced and at inconvenient times, in search of detailed answers to unformulated questions. But perhaps the situation is more likely to be improved by describing in detail the manner of approach which should be adopted rather than by enlarging on the practices which should not be followed.

The student should always remember that he is asking for help and taking the time of busy people. Many of these, as already suggested, are in no way obliged to deal with historical enquiries. There is also a limit to what officials, such as librarians, archivists and curators, should be asked to do. But whoever the person whose assistance is being sought, he will almost certainly do much more to help, if he is courteously treated, than the student has any right to expect.

Before approaching anyone, the enquirer should always make sure that he has first helped himself to the best of his ability. Many problems can be resolved in discussion with a teacher or tutor. Sensible consultation of the catalogue of the local library and of standard reference works will answer questions which are often put to officials. In the same way, the guide to the local record office will indicate the nature and scope of the documents which it contains. Preparatory work of this kind should not only enable the student to solve many of his initial problems for himself, but it should also help him to state more precisely than he otherwise could the questions which he will be asking others to answer. These questions should not be too numerous or too general.

The first request for aid should usually be by letter. The student should give his name and address, state his interest, and describe briefly what he is trying to do. Then, depending on the nature of his enquiry, he should ask if he can make an appointment to see the person concerned, consult certain material, or be given the answers to specific questions. A stamped, addressed envelope for the reply should always be enclosed with the letter. During interviews and in subsequent work in offices and private houses, common courtesy should continue to be exercised. Any rules must be strictly observed and care taken to ensure that the time and good nature of those assisting are not trespassed upon. All helpers should, of course, be thanked for their co-operation. When considerable aid has been received, a copy of any finished work might well be presented to the individual or organisation concerned as a token of gratitude and for the benefit of other investigators.

BOOKS

A. Jewell comp., *Crafts, Trades and Industries* (National Council of Social Service, 1964) is a useful booklist compiled for local historians. See also J. G. Jenkins, *Traditional Country Craftsmen* (Routledge and Kegan Paul, 1965).

A. H. Krappe, *The Science of Folklore* (Methuen, 1962) and C. S. Burne, *The Handbook of Folklore* (Folklore Society, rev. ed., 1914) are valuable surveys with extensive bibliographies. The following standard works may be specially mentioned: G. L. Gomme, *A Dictionary of British Folklore*, 2 vols. (Nutt, 1894-98); A. R. Wright, ed. T. E. Lowes, *British Calendar Customs: England*, 3 vols. (Folklore Society, 1936-40); C. Hole, *Witchcraft in England* (Batsford, 1945); and I. and P. Opie, *The Lore and Language of Schoolchildren* (Oxford, Clarendon Press, 1959).

H. Orton, *Survey of English Dialects: Introduction* (E. J. Arnold, 1962) describes the national survey being undertaken by the Department of English at the University of Leeds: some of the regional volumes have been published. Dialect dictionaries have been compiled for some counties. J. J. Wright, ed., *The English Dialect Dictionary*, 6 vols. (Oxford University Press, 1923) is still useful.

W. M. Williams has written sociological studies of two villages which are useful for both content and method, *The Sociology of an English Village: Gosforth* (Routledge and Kegan Paul, 1956) and *A West Country Village: Ashworthy* (Routledge and Kegan Paul, 1963). See also R. Frankenberg, *Communities in Britain* (Penguin Books, 1966).

Books such as Sir J. Lemon, *Reminiscences of Public Life in Southampton*, 2 vols. (Southampton, Gilbert, 1911) and G. E. Evans, *Ask the Fellows who Cut the Hay* (Faber, 1956) may be available for a specific locality, although they are rarer than might be expected. Several County Federations or individual branches of the Women's Institute have published local recollections and traditions: see, for example, M. R. Dacombe ed., *Dorset Up Along and Down Along* (3rd ed. Dorchester, Longmans, 1951).

ADDRESSES

The addresses of many useful people and organisations are listed in earlier chapters. *A Directory of Authorities and Organisations* (National Council of Social Service, 1964); S. E. Harcup comp., *Historical, Archaeological and Kindred Societies in the British Isles* (University of London, Institute of Historical Research, 1965); and *Scientific and Learned Societies of Great Britain* (Allen and Unwin, 1964) provide details of others.

LOCAL MUSEUMS, LIBRARIES AND SOCIETIES. These often have collections of relevant material, such as bygones, photographs and written records. Sometimes they also have tape recorded interviews with old inhabitants. Occasionally, in Lincolnshire, for example, formal attempts have been made to record the recollections of old people in institutions and hostels. The Department of English, University College, Gower Street, London, W.C.1. is conducting a survey of English folklore and invites local co-operation. The files of the Folk Lore Society are held at University College and include a Central Register of Folklore Research based on subject and county card-indexes. These can be consulted. The Society's publications, which include the *Folklore Journal*, contain valuable material.

THE SOCIETY FOR FOLK LIFE STUDIES publishes a journal, *Folk Life*.

THE ENGLISH FOLK DANCE AND SONG SOCIETY, CECIL SHARP HOUSE, 2, REGENT'S PARK ROAD, LONDON, N.W.1. publishes catalogues of folk song and dance books and records.

THE BRITISH DRAMA LEAGUE, 9, FITZROY SQUARE, LONDON, W.1. has produced a series of English dialect records.

Dialect recordings are often held by the regional headquarters of the B.B.C. For the national dialect survey being undertaken by the University of Leeds, see p. 114.

Part III

Local History Studies in School and College

Chapter 1 Their Place and Problems

A teacher who is interested in using local history in his work will not only need to be familiar with the main types of sources which have been described in Part II, but he will also have to consider questions of educational principle and problems of organisation. Much that he can usefully study by, and for, himself may prove to be unsuitable for, or difficult to use with, classes of pupils or individual students.

SCOPE, CONTENT AND METHODS OF WORK

Three main methods of using local history material in education have been identified in Part I. It may be introduced incidentally to illustrate national or international themes; it may take the form of a local survey; or it may consist of detailed study of an aspect or aspects of the environment. All of these approaches can be based on material which is primarily, or only partly, historical in nature. Consequently, such work may be undertaken within a History scheme; it may be linked with another subject, such as Geography; or it may form part of a broader Social or Environmental Studies approach.

Generally speaking, far less importance is at present attached to the local environment in the teaching of history than in the teaching of, for example, geography and biology. To some extent this is probably due to the fact that the historical sources are more varied and often more difficult both to acquire and to use. But, at the same time, this situation also reflects the narrowness of the traditional history syllabus which could often be usefully enlarged to include local material relating to aspects which are already taught from a national point of view as well as local topics, many of them in the field of social and economic life and history, which are frequently never even mentioned. Bearing in mind the kinds of local material described earlier, the history teacher who is going to make the fullest use of what his environment offers must be prepared to consider as history much that did not form part of his own education in that subject.

If teachers sometimes interpret the educational function and the content of history in too restricted a fashion, the reverse often applies in respect of their definition of 'local'. Thus, for many children in junior schools, local history is the history of a large city and its environs, and for many secondary school pupils it consists of aspects of the history of a whole county. It could be argued that better results would often be achieved if smaller units were studied. What, in fact, is 'local' history?

The essential value of local material in education is that it either already lies, or is about to be brought, within the real experience of the pupils. If it lacks this reality, it loses most of the advantages ascribed to it in Part I, and those which it retains are not the result of its being local. Therefore, any teacher who proposes to use local history must ensure that his material is really local for his pupils. On many occasions this will mean that the area around the school itself or a suburb will provide the basis for a more fruitful study than a whole town. Similarly, the detailed examination of a single parish or a geographical feature, such as a small river valley, may be more rewarding than superficial and largely second-hand work on half a county. A further advantage of starting work in this way is that new and unfamiliar places and topics can often be naturally linked with the results of the nearby investigations which have already been undertaken. This is important since the purpose of studying the neighbourhood will often be, not to confine attention to it, but to facilitate the extension of knowledge and experience. Sometimes the sources, methods and techniques employed in work on the immediate locality will also be deliberately used in more distant places. These may be reached by coach, perhaps, or by staying away from home. Such visits are likely to yield the best results if they have been preceded by, and are based on the same principles as, some more local investigations. The foregoing remarks are not intended to imply that a very small unit must form the basis of all local history studies: the increasing ease and frequency of travel, for example, are extending the environment of both junior and secondary school children. They are simply intended to ensure that the material which a teacher chooses to call local is also meaningfully local to his pupils.

Even if it were desirable, several reasons make it impossible, in a general book like this, to prescribe detailed syllabuses and schemes of work in local history. The opportunities offered by different localities vary; so do the ages and abilities of pupils, and the time available for study. Likewise, the objectives which teachers have in mind in studying the neighbourhood will clearly not always be the same. However, although these variables exist, the source-types and the principles governing their use remain constant. It is possible, therefore, to devise local studies to meet the needs of students of different ages many of which can, with certain modifications, be used with other age and ability groups. Accordingly, certain fundamental aspects of such work, which apply at all levels, will now be discussed, and these are followed by examples of local history studies which have been successfully completed in colleges and schools.

The list of aspects of general history which can be illustrated from a locality is usually a long one and often includes many of the following: prehistoric archaeology; life in Roman Britain; the Anglo-Saxon conquest and settlement; the conversion to Christianity; Viking invasions; the Norman Conquest and Domesday Book; life on the manor; medieval agriculture; medieval town life; markets and fairs; merchant and craft gilds; castles; monastic life; the Wars of the Roses; Tudor government; the Reformation; the Civil War; parliamentary enclosures and modern agriculture; the Industrial Revolution and modern industries; turnpike roads and coaching; canals and railways; parliamentary history and elections; political life and reforms; working-class movements; social life and reforms, such as poor laws, public health, education and leisure; local government at county, municipal corporation and parish level; architectural development; and famous people with local connections. Local history as illustration is usually the easiest method for the teacher to employ: but it is easier still for him not to use it. Thus there is abundant scope for the development of this simple technique. A few hours spent in reading some of the standard works on the history of a locality will normally yield a surprising amount of information, and lines of enquiry to pursue, relating to such themes.

Many topics like those just listed as illustrations can also be used as aspects to be studied in more detail as part of a general or a local history course. They may be treated, perhaps, as periods, events, personalities or problems. If a comprehensive chronological course is being followed, there will probably be some gaps in the local story, either because the neighbourhood played no part in a particular episode or because no suitable material concerning it survives. The gaps themselves may, of course, be significant and attention should be drawn to this. As a general rule, however, the teacher should concentrate on those subjects for which the local material is fullest and most suited to the needs of his particular pupils. He should certainly never be tempted to over-estimate the significance of any local episode.

When the approach to the past starts from the local community itself rather than from work in national history, many of the topics already listed will still be relevant, but they will probably be differently emphasised. A large number of additional topics will also present themselves in most localities. Much of this work can often be usefully studied by first considering the present situation and then investigating historical aspects. Suitable subjects for study may include, for example, the physical background, geology, soil, vegetation, land use, boundaries, settlement-patterns, names, field remains, monuments, buildings of all kinds, agriculture, industry, shops and services, transport and communications, local government, law and order, population, poverty and sickness, leisure and entertainment, planning, famous places, and famous people.

A large number of different aspects may be investigated with the same class so as to produce a local survey. Again, the content may be mainly historical or it may relate to varied aspects of the local community, past, present and future. The survey may be completed in a fairly short all-out assault or it may be spread over a longer period. Ambitious surveys have often been recommended as the most valuable form of local work. These have an educational value, but it is important to ask whether their disadvantages do not outweigh their advantages. The breadth and depth of local knowledge required, as well as the organisational problems involved, must make the full-scale survey an exceptional, rather than a typical, exercise. If the venture does not go well, the teacher may be deterred from further experiments in environmental work. If it does, will he have the time, energy and co-operation from colleagues and helpers to enable him to repeat the exercise annually?

There are not only three broad ways in which local history material can be introduced into work in schools and colleges, but also three basic methods by which students can be organised for such activities. The teacher may treat them as a class; he may arrange them in groups; or he may encourage them to produce individual studies. All approaches are used at all stages of education. Class instruction is common in schools and colleges, and this is undoubtedly the easiest way for the teacher to use his local material. Whether he is concerned with the content of local history in a junior school, local illustrations of national themes in a secondary school, or the sources of local history in a college of education, once he has gathered his material he has simply to feed it into his lessons or lectures. In such circumstances, however, the extent of the pupils' activity and involvement are likely to be limited to the completion of short, set tasks. The organisation of group and individual work in local history, as in all subjects, requires more energy and initiative on the teacher's part. The benefits which the students may derive from these activities have already been discussed and are increasingly appreciated.[1] Soundly based group work in this field is still probably most commonly found in junior schools, and individual

[1] See pp. 6-9.

studies have been especially characteristic of post-war work in colleges of education. No method, however, is restricted to a single educational level and the use of a variety of methods is likely to spread. For example, group work in colleges of education has increased since 1945 and the individual study will certainly become a marked feature of secondary school work with the recent advent of the Certificate of Secondary Education.

PLACE IN THE SYLLABUS

On what occasions in education from the junior school to the college of education is work in local history most usually undertaken at present? Where does it appear most frequently in their activities?

Local work may figure at any stage as a part of the official time-table and/or as an extra-curricular activity. While there is much to be said in favour of the latter, it needs to be recognised that, if this is the only way in which such work is experienced, then many children are automatically excluded from its benefits since not all will be able, for a variety of reasons, to take part in out-of-school activities.

Within school or college, constant use of incidental local illustrations can obviously be made within the framework of a conventional approach and syllabus. More extended studies may be undertaken on irregular, or regular, occasions, as time, knowledge and purpose allow. Irregularly, topics of national history are studied in detail from the local point of view on many occasions, and a few lessons may be devoted to topics such as items of local interest which the children bring from home and current events. The former method can develop into a systematic course based on local history which may comprise fairly formal lessons given by the teacher or which may consist of less formal group or individual studies. The irregular use of local material will usually be easy to arrange since the teacher can allocate the time which he has available to suit his requirements: the more ambitious ventures will need more forethought and may involve some manipulation of the time-table.

In the junior school, local history work is probably most commonly undertaken in the third, and especially the fourth, years. While some studies may be limited to history, it is likely that a more general approach to the environment will be used. In the secondary school, where time-tables are less fluid and the approach to education is more subject-centred, the early part of the history course or its last stages are often concerned with the locality. Thus it is not unusual to find the first term, or the first year, devoted to local history or local studies as an introduction to the study of history and other subjects or, less frequently, of the environment itself. These early secondary school studies often draw upon a wider area, are more systematic, and include and define more technical terms than previous primary school projects. They often launch the new course very successfully, but can run the risk of stealing the thunder from the work of later years. In non-grammar secondary schools, the last year's work in history, especially for pupils who are not taking external examinations, often concentrates on recent social and economic developments and civics as a preparation for entering society. The course is sometimes based on the neighbourhood and, even where it is not, there are ample opportunities for investigating local topics. This kind of work, much of which is organised on a group or individual basis, frequently introduces a more practical element into history studies which is welcomed by pupils. In the grammar school, those who stay on into the VIth form usually have the best chance of engaging in local work. Some history specialists, though still far too few, study a local topic as an extra in order to familiarise themselves with historical method. Pupils following a general course may also study local history, most frequently as one aspect of an elementary social survey which they sometimes undertake.

Until recently external examinations in history have done little to encourage the study of the locality and, with their emphasis on the reproduction of memorised national factual information, a great deal to discourage it. It is significant that no G.C.E. Board has provided opportunities for submitting the results of field work in history comparable to the practice in geography, for example. Since the mid-fifties, however, some examining bodies have tried to promote local study in secondary modern schools. Thus, both the content of the syllabus and the types of question set by the Union of Educational Institutions have encouraged local work and so, even more directly, have the syllabuses of the Union of Lancashire and Cheshire Institutes. The Certificate of Secondary Education, introduced in 1964, with its emphasis on, for instance, teacher control, examining on a school's own syllabus, and course work, could revolutionise the teaching of history and lead to a very great increase in local studies. But it is too early yet to assess its real impact. Meanwhile, it is perhaps worth remarking that in junior schools, and even more in secondary schools of all types, some of the most interesting, if not the only, extensive local studies which are pursued, are carried out in the period after the external examinations have been completed and when 'real work' is finished.

Students following various courses in colleges of education engage in local history studies. They include students of main subjects, such as history and geography; those who are likely to teach history in junior and secondary schools; and many following the Education course for whom an acquaintance with the resources of the neighbourhood will be useful. While particular specialised courses may be held at various times and much incidental local material may be used continuously throughout, lectures and group work on the locality often come early in the three-year course as an introduction to a new approach to knowledge and methods of work, both general and historical. The major piece of local study which is produced by history students is normally a long essay, often called an individual study or a thesis. This need not concern a local subject, but since it is often stipulated that the student must use primary source materials, it very often does, because this is the field where they are most readily available. Whether these essays and similar ones which are written as part of another main subject or Education course, always achieve their aims is questionable, a point which will be considered later.

Outside the curriculum in both school and college, local history is pursued both informally by groups and individuals and more formally by societies. Provided that the teacher is willing to give up his time, there are endless opportunities for promoting interest amongst a limited number of pupils. After-school meetings, Saturday, week-end and holiday visits are devoted to activities such as indoor meetings with speakers, visits to sites and buildings, and field work. Various clubs and societies have programmes which may be partly or entirely local historical in character: they include historical, archaeological, architectural, rambling, cycling, photographic and field study groups.

That a considerable amount of work in local history goes on, particularly at the times indicated, proves that such studies are possible under present conditions. Much more could be done at these same and other levels, and even more still would be possible were history syllabuses in general concerned more with training thinking citizens and less with producing crammers of factual information. One reason why local history studies have not developed to a greater extent may lie in the concentration of effort in many colleges of education on the individual study. Normally this introduces the student to only a very limited number of sources and considers them mainly from an academic point of view. In such circumstances, the student never experiences himself what he should later be asking his pupils to do: more time could often usefully be given in colleges to group work on local projects and to considering the educational relevance of that kind of activity. If this were done it could well result in less emphasis being placed on the separate subject approach, and the educational advantages of environmental work could become as apparent to all teachers as they already have to the teachers of many young, and most backward, pupils.

ORGANISATIONAL PROBLEMS

There are certain organisational aspects of local history work, especially where pupils are actively engaged, which, present practice suggests, deserve comment and improvement. Moreover, if the amount of local work other than the incidental use of illustration by the teacher is going to increase, then it is essential that proper attention is paid to these practical points. They are discussed here in the three main stages into which local work can be broadly divided.

Planning and Preparation.

Many of the books which have been written about local studies exhort the teacher and his students to explore their environment together, discovering as they go. This method may sometimes produce satisfactory results within a limited field, but it is far more likely to lead to dead ends, wasted time, and frustration. In the writer's experience, the success of local work with students of all ages is normally closely related to the amount of careful preparation which the teacher has undertaken beforehand. This is not to say that the pupils will not be making discoveries: they will, and to better effect than they otherwise might, because the teacher, striking a careful balance between under and over direction, is unobtrusively guiding the broad lines of their enquiries.

The kind of planning and preparation which the teacher will need to do will vary, of course, with the type of project which he has in mind. If, for example, he wishes to illustrate his lessons on Roman Britain by referring to the Roman occupation locally, he will have to be sufficiently familiar with the general history of the conquest and settlement to know what may be reflected in the neighbourhood, and he must then search libraries and museums for relevant information. If he intends that his pupils should investigate selected aspects of the locality, he will first need to explore the area himself in order to assess its possibilities. He will have to decide how much time can be spent on the work and determine what is valuable and interesting to, and within the capabilities of, his pupils. He must locate sources and estimate their value, and he must make contact with people who may be able, and willing, to help. He must also appreciate the inter-relationships which may be established and the follow-up themes which could emerge. This kind of preliminary survey by the organiser of local work is essential at whatever level the latter is being conducted, and one of the present weaknesses of many investigations is the absence of just such an assessment. Consequently, lacking adequate initial direction, children's exploration of an area or students' individual studies are often not as good as they might, and should, be. It is easy to have bright ideas about what one would like to do and then, as the work progresses, to discover that it cannot be done because either the local evidence is scarce or it is too difficult to use. It is much more profitable to find out broadly what material is available and what possibilities for study it offers before the general lines of an investigation are laid down. This work of preparation and planning, elementary or complex, becomes much easier as experience grows since the source types and the difficulties which they present, as well as the purely organisational problems, remain basically the same, while the lessons learned from each piece of work are valuable in all subsequent investigations.

The necessity of correctly interpreting the word 'local' has already been emphasised. Natural, political or arbitrary units may equally well provide the framework of a study, so that a valley, a parish, a ward, or a circle around the school, for instance, could constitute satisfactory areas for enquiries on particular occasions. The essential characteristic of the local material is that it must relate to places already within, or which are capable of being brought within, the pupils' experience. The purpose of the work should also be correctly assessed from the outset. Too many local history studies at present seem to be based on the assumption that, in the course of them, important historical discoveries ought to be made: to a greater or lesser degree, there is an emphasis on 'original research'. It is true that significant discoveries may sometimes be made and, if they are, they should certainly be recorded for general information. But the prime reason for studying the neighbourhood, whether as a junior school project, C.S.E. essay or college of education individual study, will normally lie, not in the research results, but in the effect which the exercise has on those participating. In this work, teachers need to make sure that limited and manageable local materials are being used for well-defined educational purposes.

It is usually a good idea to have a central theme or themes

for local studies. These can often be usefully posed as a problem or series of problems. In this way, there are questions to be answered and the facts discovered come to be treated as evidence: yardsticks are provided by which the value of information can be measured, thus preventing much side-tracking and mere rag-bag compilation.

Besides preparing himself the teacher will also need to prepare his pupils for local work. They may need to have special knowledge before they can adequately perform certain tasks; they may need to master techniques, such as map reading; they may need practice in methods of recording and citing authorities; they may need instruction in how to behave when out of school and how to ask people for help. Such matters should not be over-stressed in the abstract or boredom will soon set in; at the same time training in such aspects and emphasis on high standards are essential in all this kind of work.

Collecting and Recording

Preparatory planning should ensure that the topics upon which pupils will work and the main sources which they will be consulting are suited to their needs and abilities. Many practical problems will still be encountered, however, as the work unfolds and progresses. This will be true even where relatively mature and able students are working on individual studies: it applies with even more force to the activities of an average class of children organised on a group basis. Many teachers advance these difficulties as the reason for their being unable to engage in any local work. That such problems may cause complications cannot be denied: but neither can the fact that a large number of teachers successfully overcome them.

Many of these difficulties are connected with going out of school and apply to all local work. History is merely meeting them later than have some other subjects and history teachers ought to be benefiting from their experience. Local Authorities are often said to make work outside school difficult. Circular 140 concerning school visits and payments by L.E.A.'s has certainly been variously interpreted since it was issued in 1947. In some places considerable notice needs to be given when children are to be taken out of school during schooltime. Many Authorities, however, have long taken an enlightened view of extra-mural activities and, since the publication of the Newsom Report in 1963, enthusiasm has increased. It is likely that the realisation of the value of field work and visits will continue to spread, but, if it does not, there is no reason why teachers should not educate administrators in this respect. Headteachers, too, sometimes need convincing that local studies are worthwhile. Undoubtedly, the surest advertisement is to undertake some very limited projects as a beginning, to convert the doubters, and then to proceed to bigger schemes.

The time-table is often quoted as an insurmountable barrier, especially in secondary schools. The first point to establish in this connection is that the amount of time which needs to be spent out of school is normally a very small proportion of the total allocated to a particular project. An occasional half-day can be very valuable and so, too, is the double period at the end of an afternoon. If insufficient school time is available it may be possible for material to be collected on the journey to and from school, at the week-ends, or in the holidays. Restriction on the number of children, often twenty, to be accompanied out of school by a single adult, is also often held to impede local work. Certainly, if the teacher himself cannot take all his class, then another adult must be found either to go with him or to take charge of those of his children who stay in school. More co-operation amongst staff would often help; and students on teaching practice can both contribute to such work and learn from it. Parental assistance might also be sought much more frequently than it is. Questions of transport and money to pay for items, such as materials and fares, also have to be faced, but are in no way insuperable.

It is not as difficult then to work out of school as is sometimes claimed. Nevertheless, it must be emphasised that all such work needs to be carefully organised and directed. Perhaps one of the biggest hindrances to the development of soundly based extra-mural activities is still the attitude of many teachers that going out constitutes a 'treat' and must be indulged in only occasionally and always on a grand scale.

There are various ways in which pupils may collect information outside the classroom which broadly correspond with practice inside. They may be taken on a coach tour of an area or a conducted tour of a building, ruin or museum, and be told what they are seeing. This method may be useful, for example, as a preparation for more detailed work or to increase specialised vocabulary, but it makes few demands upon the pupils apart from frequently asking them to remember too much unrelated, detailed information. Alternatively, they may be left to ask questions as they go around, efforts being made, where necessary, to lead them towards asking those which are significant. This is a difficult technique to practise, especially if the group is large. Often the best method is for students to be working individually or in pairs or groups on prepared assignments. Such assignments may be based on the filling-in of questionnaires, the completion of maps, the making or annotating of drawings or diagrams, or the collection of specimens, for instance. The devising of these tasks should often be undertaken with the co-operation of the pupils who, as already suggested, will need some training for their investigations. It may be desirable to plan work to and from the main site which is to be visited. Work on the site should not last too long: pupils should be kept busy, but should also be allowed some time for browsing and relaxation. Details such as feeding and toilet arrangements and what to do if the weather is wet should never be overlooked.

The chief sources which pupils may be using in their local history studies can be viewed in four main groups: these are the field and material remains; maps; books and documents; and people. Where different types of sources are going to be consulted in a specific investigation, it is often important to consider the best order in which they might be used. At all levels of education, it is not uncommon for the real thing to be examined only after it has been read about in detail: there are many occasions when this sequence could be usefully reversed. The tasks which pupils are set to do on all types of source material must also be considered more carefully than they sometimes are at present. As a result of the preliminary enquiries which he has carried out, the teacher will be able to make sure that he is setting well-defined and limited tasks which his pupils will be able to complete. He will also be able to indicate where and how the necessary information can be found. In recent years, there has been far too much aimless, general searching, involving disappointment and frustration for pupils and the wasting of time by public servants and private people who have often been pestered with general and undefined requests for information.

The field and material remains should present few major difficulties in their use provided that attention is paid to the points which have already been discussed. A relevant service, already provided by several Local Authorities, which could be usefully extended is the school loans service. Under this scheme various items, which often include archaeological specimens, maps and pictures, are lent to schools for teaching purposes, thus making it unnecessary to leave the school premises in order to use them. The chief problem raised by maps, once they can be read, is their expense. Various ways of economising in their use, however, will soon be discovered. Maps for educational purposes, bought direct from the Ordnance Survey, are subject to appreciable discount. A single sheet can often be cut into several pieces for group work: if it is necessary to see the relationship between pieces as the work is in progress they can be hung against the background of another whole sheet. Sketch maps can be duplicated easily and cheaply by a variety of processes. Extensive tracing is unnecessary and should be avoided.

Books for local history work often constitute the biggest problem of all. Many new areas of interest are likely to be opened up for the teacher where his own knowledge of published material is scanty. Moreover, the books which he eventually locates and consults for himself will normally be of use only to older and brighter pupils. Two kinds of books on which children can work are needed in local studies. The first are junior reference books on national topics which figure in the story of the neighbourhood, for example, Anglo-Saxon England, the parish church or railways. The supply of such books has improved enormously in the last twenty years, and most major topics are now at least adequately covered. The same cannot be said of the second kind, books containing local information. In some areas, especially large towns, local history publications designed for children have been produced and there is room for many more of these. But all too often pupils will be obliged to obtain their information from books which were written for adults. The transcription or paraphrasing by the teacher of passages from rare books which cannot be brought into the classroom or detailed direction of the children to specific pages of difficult works may be necessary. The compilation of children's booklets may also be desirable. All this clearly takes time, and one of the best ways to further local studies lies in the extension of co-operative ventures in the production of such material. Some examples of publications of this nature are given later. Several of these reproduce or refer to local documents. The problems presented by documentary material are in many ways the same as those raised by other written sources though they may appear in a more acute form. The most urgent need is that groups of teachers should confer with local archivists, librarians and curators, for the former seldom know what is available and usable by children, while the latter are ignorant of the teacher's detailed needs.

People, either the teacher or outside helpers, will often supply information which cannot be obtained easily, or at all, from any other source. The outsiders may be public officials or private persons who, as already mentioned, are often pleased to help provided that they are not troubled too frequently and are asked specific, sensible questions.[1] Here again the importance of pupils being clear about what they want to learn from a person would seem to be obvious. Even so, a great deal of resentment has been caused in recent years by students of all ages who have approached a great variety of persons in a discourteous manner, having done little or nothing to help themselves, and with unformulated enquiries. If the assistance of outside persons is going to be sought, it must

[1] See pp. 110-114.

be for reasonable, limited and well-defined help. It is also sometimes wise for the teacher to explain briefly to a person who is going to be interviewed just why the children are consulting him.

Presentation of Results and Follow-Up

Some local investigations may illustrate general themes which have already been established; some may be complete in themselves; some may be designed to lead on to other studies. The results of all have to be presented and, from most of them, certain explicit lessons have to be drawn. This final stage suffers on some occasions because too little time is left for it and, on others, because too much effort is devoted to over-elaborate presentation. More adequate planning and preparation could prevent both faults.

In producing finished results, the interest, impressions and material collected in the form of rough notes, completed questionnaires, sketch maps, drawings and so on have to be consolidated and re-presented. The methods chosen for recording a particular project will probably depend to some extent on the nature and purpose of that specific investigation. Some remarks which are of general application can, however, be made. One of the advantages of local work lies in the variety of recording techniques which can be utilised. There are plenty of opportunities for written work, factual and imaginative, prose and poetry. Indeed, a criticism which might be made of the presentation of some results is that too much use is made of the written, especially the narrative, record. Maps, plans, charts, sketches, drawings, paintings, diagrams, photographs and models may frequently be more appropriate. Oral work can also be naturally developed. If the work is designed, as many individual studies are, primarily as a written academic exercise, then more care should be taken than often is to ensure that all irrelevant material is excluded and that something more than simple description is achieved.

It has often been suggested that local work in school, especially a local survey, should culminate in an exhibition of work done. While an exhibition may sometimes form a useful goal at which to aim, this recommendation has often had the unfortunate effect of linking local work too closely with events like Open Days. Neighbourhood investigations have thus been seen as extraordinary ventures to be indulged in only as large-scale exercises on special occasions.

For local history to contribute most usefully to education, the opposite advice is necessary. The teacher should start in a small way, building up a store of local knowledge and meeting practical problems gradually. As experience and confidence grow he should aim to become a lively opportunist who is able to realise and utilise quickly the potentialities of any environment. He is also likely to be most successful if he does not work in isolation. The development of local studies would be greatly facilitated and encouraged in all areas if teacher-groups were formed to discover and disseminate source material and to discuss particular pieces of work which had been carried out. While much of this work would rightly continue to be essentially historical in origin and scope, there is little doubt that, as greater understanding and proficiency were acquired, the environment itself, as well as academic subjects, would increasingly become the starting point and focus for many investigations.

Chapter 2 Examples of Local History Studies

In the following accounts practising teachers describe work in local history which they have undertaken at various levels.

All the examples concern places in Dorset, Hampshire and West Sussex because the writer has intimate knowledge of the colleges and schools in that area. The reasons for using illustrations based on personally-known projects are obvious: they are relatively easy to obtain and their details are authentic and to the point. The only possible disadvantage in drawing them from a restricted area is that it may then be argued that such activities cannot necessarily be pursued in other regions. This argument is, in fact, false. School environments throughout the country are basically rural, urban or suburban in character: it is simply the numbers of a particular type which may vary considerably from region to region. Moreover, the main sources, methods and techniques of local work remain broadly the same in whatever area a particular kind of environment occurs. Accordingly, many diverse ways of using local history in a variety of neighbourhoods are reproduced here in the hope that they will convince teachers of the practicability of such work and encourage them to discover similar, and other, opportunities in their own localities. Many of the principles underlying work of this kind are also explicit or implicit in these descriptions.

Since this book has been written primarily for teachers in colleges and departments of education and in junior and secondary schools, all the examples describe work which has been carried out in these establishments. It is important to notice, however, that many of the projects attempted at the stage described could well be used, with certain modifications, at either of the other levels. Moreover, all the examples quoted are relevant to education in independent schools, and many of them could also be applied to work with further education, undergraduate and extra-mural students.

It has already been shown that all work in local history can be broadly classified as lessons or lectures, group work, and individual studies, and that any of these may be organised within the college or school time-table or as an extra-curricular activity. The varied scope of such work has also been emphasised, embracing, as it does, simple illustration of national history, detailed studies of aspects of the neighbourhood and local surveys. The case studies show the main approaches in operation at the various levels. Few accounts of courses of formal lessons have been included because they are the easiest to envisage and to practise. All the examples relate to the environment which is local to the college or school itself, but the technique can be practised equally well away from the home area.

Examples of work in teacher-training institutions are given first and are followed by those from junior, and then, secondary schools. The teacher-training section opens with an account of work on a village: the approach, techniques and sources are described in detail because they are relevant to many local studies at all levels. Descriptions are then given of lecture-courses, individual studies, group work and informal activities which have been conducted with students in training and with practising teachers. In both junior and secondary school sections examples of work carried out mainly within the school time-table precede out of school activities, and those which are based on relatively limited topics come before more extensive investigations. In all the sub-divisions a broad chronological arrangement has been adopted.

A standard lay-out is used for the individual descriptions except for a few where this was impossible or undesirable. The name of the school or college and the teacher or teachers involved and the title of the project are given first, and these are followed by a statement of the purpose of the exercise, the time devoted to it, and an account of the work itself together with the teacher's retrospective comments on it.

(i) TEACHER-TRAINING INSTITUTIONS

(a) University of Southampton Institute of Education.

Mr. R. Douch and
Mr. J. G. Rushby.

Introduction to Sources of Local History.

Twenty to thirty graduate students working for the Certificate in Education or practising teachers attending short courses.

The objects of this work, based on the rural parish of Amberley in West Sussex, were to introduce students to as many types of sources of local history as possible, to indicate some of the opportunities which the environment may present for work with children, and to illustrate methods of work and techniques relevant to such studies. The coverage and treatment of both topics and sources is not, of course, exhaustive. In particular, it should be mentioned that one of the purposes of the work was to show what could be achieved using as written sources only those which were available in print: much could be added if readily accessible unpublished documents, such as manorial and parish records and enclosure and tithe maps, were also consulted. It was emphasised that this project was not intended to be a blueprint of work which might be undertaken with children: teachers should select particular aspects of their locality or community for study with their classes and should modify the approach to them as might be necessary. Similar studies of other rural and urban areas have been undertaken. Where possible, students investigate both a village and what seems, at first sight, to be a most unpromising suburban district.

The time spent investigating the settlement and subsequently in lectures and discussions varies according to circumstances: a frequent pattern is described below.

Amberley (O.S. 2½ in. map, Sheet TQ 01), five miles north

of Arundel, was chosen for study simply because it is situated conveniently near centres where courses are frequently held. It is an old and attractive agricultural settlement, now taken over to a large extent by London commuters and retired people. The tutors studied the locality, considered its possibilities, investigated sources, and devised the assignment sheets which are reproduced later in this section. These fall into two groups, field work sheets (marked A.F.) and sheets based on written sources (marked A.L.).

The course opened with a brief introduction explaining the aims and organisation of the work and asking that results should be presented in as visual a form as possible, with maps, charts, diagrams and models. The tutors then led the party round the survey area looking at it from vantage points and posing significant questions. One or occasionally two field work sheets, with their explicit instructions and any necessary maps and materials, were then distributed to pairs of students who spent four or five hours collecting their information. Later, approximately the same time was occupied by the same pairs working on written material. Most of this was gathered together at a convenient centre to save time and, where possible, students pursued topics similar, or related, to those which they had investigated in the field. On both occasions tutors were present to deal with questions or difficulties as they arose. The finished work of each pair, based on all the sources used, was subsequently displayed and members reported to the group on the nature of their assignments and discoveries, the sources consulted, any problems encountered, and the methods employed to present their information. As the discussion proceeded, slides were shown to remind students of relevant features and, when it had finished, another visit was made to the survey area. Lectures followed on sources and on local work in school, and all had an opportunity to study and discuss aspects of the project with which they had not been directly concerned.

The Amberley sheets, arranged in the following order of discussion, illustrate the theme, 'Rock and Man: the influence of rock structure and relief on the history of a community': A.F.1, A.L.2, A.F.2, A.L.1, A.F.3, A.L.3, A.F.4, A.F.5, A.F.6,

A.F.9, A.F.13, A.F.14, A.F.15, A.L.8, A.F.16, A.F.17, A.F.7, A.L.4, A.L.6, A.L.7, A.F.8, A.L.5, A.L.9, A.F.11, A.L.11, A.L.10, A.F.10, A.L.12, A.F.12, A.L.13, A.L.14, A.L.15, A.L.16, A.L.17, A.L.18, A.L.19, A.L.20, A.L.21, A.L.22, A.L.23. In this way the geological and geographical background is surveyed and aspects of the present settlement, with a certain amount of historical background, are then considered. Prehistoric remains are identified, the parish delineated and three aspects of history pursued—influential local people, the community as a whole, and agricultural changes. No detailed account is included here of the local information discovered since the topics investigated and the methods of work employed are the features of general interest.

Field Work: Assignment Sheets.

Geology, Relief and Drainage (1). A.F.1.

1. Where possible, and with the aid of the 1 in. to 1 ml. geological map, examine the characteristics of the chief rock types: Chalk (Upper, Middle, Lower), Upper Greensand, Gault, Alluvium. Collect specimens, if you can, noting the map reference of the source of each specimen. Make field sketches of any exposures.
2. Examine the type of relief associated with each of the above rocks, particularly the north and west edges of the Upper Greensand outcrop. Make field sketches of any particularly interesting relief features.

Geology, Relief and Drainage (2). A.F.2.

1. Investigate the water courses marked on the 2½ ins. to 1 ml. O.S. map immediately to the south of Amberley village. Comment on their width and depth, direction of flow, material in suspension, etc.
2. Observe the Arun at some conveniently accessible point. Estimate its width, depth and speed of flow.
3. Examine the state of artificial drainage in Amberley Wild Brooks. Can you find out anything about its construction and development?
4. In what ways is the river Arun of commercial importance to the village?

Soils and Uncultivated Vegetation. A.F.3.

1. Make a survey of soils along the road and path from Downs Farm (035123) to 031134. Find out as much as possible about the depth, texture and quality of the soil. Collect specimens, noting the grid reference of the source of each specimen. Sketch the soil profile exposed near Downs Farm.
2. Examine and comment on uncultivated vegetation you find in a typical square yard (a) near Downs Farm, (b) near point 031134. (Make a quadrate with four wooden pegs and string.)
3. Record and comment on the types of trees and plants in the hedgerows and ditches along the road and path from Downs Farm to 031134 near changes in the surface rock indicated on the geological map. Collect specimens from the tree, shrub and ground layers. If you cannot identify any specimens, take samples and try to identify them by reference to one of the standard works available in the library.

Land Utilisation. A.F.4.

Make a survey of the area outlined in green on the map provided (6 ins. to 1 ml.), noting the use to which each plot is put. Colour the finished map as follows: arable land, brown; permanent grass, green; productive gardens, orchards, nurseries, blue; woodland, green with a tree symbol; heath and rough pasture, yellow; land agriculturally unproductive, red. With arable land, print over the colour the name of the crop; with woodland, indicate the type of trees. With agriculturally unproductive land, indicate the use to which the land is put.

Farm Study: Amberley Castle Farm: (visit arranged). A.F.5.

1. On the 6 ins. to 1 ml. O.S. map provided, outline the boundaries of the farm lands. Describe, in general terms, the location of any fields which lie off your map.
2. Who (a) owns (b) occupies the farm?
3. Can you discover anything about its history?
4. Draw a plan showing the layout of the buildings: enter the name of each and the use to which it is put.

5. Insert the letter G on all permanent pasture and long ley.
6. Name the crop to be grown this year on each of the arable fields.
7. What is the total acreage of the farm, and the acreage under arable, permanent grass, long ley, rough pasture, copse, etc.?
8. What rotations are usually used on the farm?
9. What breeds, and how many, of the various types of live-stock are kept?
10. What is the labour force? What is the degree of mech-anisation?
11. To what markets are crops and other products sent? What methods of transport are used in this connection?
12. Note any other interesting information about farming methods; effects of soils, drainage and aspect on crop-ping; weather difficulties; water supply, etc.

Industry: Amberley Chalk and Lime Works: (visit arranged). A.F.6.

Find out what you can about: the chalk beds which are quarried; the methods of quarrying used; the processing which takes place at the works; the products and their uses; methods of marketing and chief markets; transport employed; and labour force.

Parish and Settlement. A.F.7.

1. Examine the shape of Amberley parish on the 2½ ins. to 1 ml. O.S. map. How far is its boundary formed by natural features?
2. Examine the pattern of settlement in relation to relief.
3. What is the shape of the village?
4. List and comment on the significance of any names (natural features, roads, farms, houses, etc.).

Earthworks. A.F.8.

The 2½ in. and 6 in. O.S. maps show certain earthworks and stones on Amberley Mount. Locate these on the ground and draw a sketch map of their positions. Sketch the earthworks.

1. What do you think these earthworks represent?

2. What do you think the stones represent?
3. Why are they all to be found in such a remote position?

Buildings Survey. A.F.9.

1. On the outline sketch map (25 ins. to 1 ml.) provided, record the distribution of different materials used in the village for (a) walls, (b) roofs. Sketch in on your map any buildings not marked.
2. Why have these different building materials been used and where did they come from?
3. On a second outline map, try to classify the buildings according to age, using the following periods: (a) before 1700, (b) 1700-1850, (c) 1850-1944, (d) 1945 to present day. Sketch in on your map any buildings not marked.
4. Sketch interesting architectural details for each period represented. (Exclude the church and castle.)
5. Note any houses of special interest and find out what you can about them.

The Church. A.F.10.

1. How is the church sited in relation to (a) the castle, (b) the village?
2. Is there any significance in these relationships?
3. From your knowledge of architecture, can you suggest the approximate date at which the church was built? Make a rough plan of the church and sketch any particularly interesting architectural features.
4. Of what is the church built?
5. Why do you think these particular materials were used?
6. Notice the tombstones in the churchyard. Do they differ in different centuries? If so, in what ways?
7. Is the parson at Amberley a Rector or a Vicar? What is the difference between the two?

The Castle. A.F.11.

1. How is the castle sited in relation to (a) the church, (b) the village?
2. Does its position seem to be defensively a strong one?
3. What would you say the castle guards?
4. Does the building look much like a castle?

5. From your knowledge of architecture, could you suggest the approximate date at which it was built?
6. Of what is it built?
7. Draw a rough plan of the castle and sketch any architectural details which seem of interest.
8. Can you discover anything about its past and present ownership?

The School. A.F.12.

1. When was the school built, and by what body or individual?
2. Of what is it built? Sketch any interesting features.
3. What is the present status of the school under the 1944 Education Act?
4. What is the age-range of the children attending the school? How many are there on the roll? Is the number increasing or decreasing?
5. What is the catchment area of the school?
6. How many teachers are there in addition to the head? Does the head live in a school house?
7. What other schools are attended by pupils from Amberley? How do they get there?

Shops and Services. A.F.13.

1. On an outline sketch map (25 ins. to 1 ml.) provided, plot:
   (a) the location and type of shops, inns, cafés, etc.
   (b) the location and type of any general services such as builder and carpenter, and of personal services such as doctor and hairdresser.
2. What other places are used as shopping and amusement centres, and to what extent?
3. What local newspapers circulate in the village?
4. What conclusions about the village can you draw from this information?

Communications: Roads. A.F.14.

1. Relate the roads to relief in the parish.
2. Examine the time-table of buses serving Amberley. What larger centres are connected directly to it by bus?

What is the frequency of the buses? Is this the same throughout the day? Is it the same on weekdays and Sundays? Does any weekday have a more frequent service than others? If so, why? What conclusions can you draw from this information about bus services?

3. For a period of an hour, make a census of the traffic passing in both directions along the main road. Record the number of lorries, delivery vans, coaches and buses, private cars, motor cycles, cycles, farm implements. Observe, where possible, and note the origin and/or destination of vehicles.
4. Is any use made of the Arun as a means of communication?

Communications: Railway. A.F.15.

1. Relate the railway to relief in the parish.
2. Examine the time-table of trains serving Amberley. What larger centres are connected to it directly by train? What is the frequency of the trains? Is this the same throughout the day? Is it the same on weekdays and Sundays? Does any weekday have a more frequent service than others? If so, why? What conclusions can you draw from this information about train services?

Amberley Today (1). A.F.16.

1. How is the village governed?
2. What kind of people serve on this governing body?
3. How is the governing body related to the larger units of local government in the county?

Amberley Today (2). A.F.17.

1. How influential is the Castle in village life?
2. How influential is the Church?
3. What are the chief occupations of the inhabitants?
4. Is there a large retired population in the village?
5. Do many people travel out of the village daily to work? If so, where do they go?
6. Are relations between the farming community and the invaders good?
7. Do many people come into the village daily to work? If so, at what jobs?

8. Are there any particular problems or aspects of life in Amberley which you consider worthy of mention?

Written Sources: Assignment Sheets.

Geology, Relief and Drainage (1). A.L.1.

1. From the 2½ ins. to 1 ml. O.S. map, make a tracing of the parish of Amberley to show (a) the 25 ft., 100 ft., 200 ft., 300 ft., contours, (b) the drainage.
2. On a tracing of the 2½ ins. to 1 ml. map, make and colour an approximate enlargement of the part of the 1 in. to 1 ml. geological map which covers the parish of Amberley.
3. Superimpose 1 on 2.
4. Comment on any relationships thus revealed.

1 in. to 1 ml. Geological Survey Map, Sheet 317 (Drift), and 2½ ins. to 1 ml. O.S. Map, Sheet TQ 01.
F. H. Edmunds, *The Wealden District* (Geological Survey, Handbook of British Regional Geology, 3rd ed., H.M.S.O., 1954).
C. Reid, *The Geology of the Country near Chichester* (Geological Survey, H.M.S.O., 1903).
F. H. Edmunds, *The Wells and Springs of Sussex* (Geological Survey, H.M.S.O., 1928).

Geology, Relief and Drainage (2). A.L.2.

1. Prepare a brief note on each of the main rock types in the parish.
2. From the 2½ ins. to 1 ml. O.S. map and using a vertical scale of 1 in. to 400 ft., draw a section from 035100 to 035150. On your section mark in the different geological outcrops and deposits.

1 in. to 1 ml. Geological Survey Map, Sheet 317 (Drift), and 2½ ins. to 1 ml. O.S. Map, Sheet TQ 01.
F. H. Edmunds, *The Wealden District* (Handbook of British Regional Geology, 3rd ed., H.M.S.O., 1954).
C. Reid, *The Geology of the Country near Chichester* (Geological Survey, H.M.S.O., 1903).
S. W. Wooldridge and F. Goldring, *The Weald* (Collins, 1953).

Soils and Uncultivated Vegetation. A.L.3.

1. What can you find out about the soils of Amberley parish?
2. To what extent do the soils correspond to the geology of the parish?
3. What can you find out about the uncultivated vegetation of the parish?
4. Is this vegetation related closely to the soils?

Maps and books by Edmunds, Reid, Wooldridge and Goldring, as in A.L.1 and A.L.2.

A. Briault, *Sussex* (Land Utilisation Survey Report, 1942).

A. Hall and E. J. Russell, *The Agriculture and Soils of Kent, Surrey and Sussex* (H.M.S.O., 1911).

R. H. B. Jesse, *A Survey of the Agriculture of Sussex* (Royal Agricultural Society of England, 1960).

Parish Shapes and Settlement. A.L.4.

1. Trace the boundaries of the parishes of Amberley, Bury and Houghton from the 1 in. map.
2. Can you suggest why these parishes should be shaped like this?
3. How are the shape and site of the village of Amberley related to the relief and to rock types?

1 in. to 1 ml. Geological Survey Map, Sheet 317 (Drift), and 1 in. to 1 ml. O.S. Map, Sheet 182.

V. Bonham-Carter, *The English Village* (Penguin Books, 1952), pp. 98-124.

Prehistoric Earthworks. A.L.5.

1. What are the earthworks on the Downs at Amberley?
2. Why were they sited in this position?
3. When was the site abandoned?
4. Are these earthworks unusual or are they typical of Sussex?

6 ins. to 1 ml. O.S. Map, Sheet TQ 01SW.

E. C. Curwen, *Prehistoric Sussex* (The Homeland Association, 1929).

E. C. Curwen, *The Archaeology of Sussex* (2nd ed., Methuen, 1954).

Place Names. A.L.6.

1. What does the name 'Amberley' mean?
2. What information of historical interest can you derive from a study of the minor place names of the parish?
   A. Mawer and F. M. Stenton, *The Place Names of Sussex*, part i (English Place Name Society, Cambridge University Press, 1929).

Eighteenth and Early Nineteenth Century Settlement. A.L.7.

1. On three of the sketch maps provided (2½ ins. to 1 ml.) show the information relating to the parish of Amberley contained in the maps of Sussex by (a) Budgen, 1724, (b) Yeakell and Gardner, 1778-83, and (c) Greenwood, 1825.
2. Compare your prepared maps with the modern 2½ ins. to 1 ml. O.S. map of the parish and comment on any changes which have taken place.

Communications. A.L.8.

1. What can you discover about the Arun Canal?
2. When was the railway constructed? When were local stations opened?
   C. Hadfield, *The Canals of Southern England* (Phoenix House, 1955).
   C. F. D. Marshall, *History of the Southern Railway*, 2 vols. (2nd ed., I. Allan, 1963).
   H. Allcroft, *Waters of Arun* (Methuen, 1930).
   Articles on the canal in *Sussex County Magazine*, March and July, 1956.

Famous People. A.L.9.

Have any famous people lived in Amberley parish? Write brief notes on them, with particular reference to any influence which they may have had on the parish.
J. Dallaway and E. Cartwright, *A History of the Western Division of Sussex*, 2 vols. (London, 1815-32).
T. W. Horsfield, *The History, Antiquities and Topography of Sussex*, 2 vols. (Lewes, Baxter, 1835).
M. A. Lower, *A Compendious History of Sussex*, 2 vols. (Lewes, Bacon, 1870).

F. G. Brabant (rev. R. F. Jessup), *Sussex* (Methuen, Little Guide, 1957).

M. A. Lower, *The Worthies of Sussex* (Lewes, Bacon, 1865).

Lords of the Manor. A.L.10.

What can you discover about the owners of the manor of Amberley? Do not give too much detail about particular owners.

County histories as in A.L.9.

G. A. Clarkson, 'Notes on Amberley', *Sussex Archaeological Collections*, vol. xvii.

The Castle. A.L.11.

1. What is its general position and plan?
2. Was it a castle?
3. When was it built?
4. Who owned it?
5. Why was it built?
6. Draw a plan of the castle.

County histories as in A.L.9.

W. D. Peckham, 'Amberley Castle', *Sussex Archaeological Collections*, vol. lxii: good.

G. A. Clarkson, 'Notes on Amberley', *Sussex Archaeological Collections*, vol. xvii: use with care.

D. G. C. Elwes, *Castles, Mansions and Manors of West Sussex* (Longmans, 1876).

The Church. A.L.12.

1. How long has there been a church in Amberley?
2. Why is it so close to the castle?
3. What are its chief architectural features?
4. In what ways did the parish church in the Middle Ages play a larger part in the life of parishioners than it does now?

County histories as in A.L.9.

G. A. Clarkson, 'Notes on Amberley', *Sussex Archaeological Collections*, vol. xvii.

R. H. Nibbs and M. A. Lower, *The Churches of Sussex* (Brighton and Worthing, Smith, 1872).

A. H. Peat and L. C. Halstead, *Churches and other Antiquities of West Sussex* (Chichester, Moore, 1912).
F. Harrison, *Notes on Sussex Churches* (4th ed., Hove, Combridge, 1920).
V. Bonham-Carter, *The English Village* (Penguin Books, 1952), pp. 161-200.

Amberley in 1086. A.L.13.

1. Read the account of Domesday Book for Sussex: copy the extract relating to Amberley: analyse the information.
2. Try to relate the extract to the Amberley entry in W. D. Parish, *Domesday Book Facsimile for Sussex*.
   Victoria County History, Sussex, vol. i, pp. 351-451.
   W. D. Parish, *Domesday Book Facsimile for Sussex* (Lewes, Wolff, 1886).

Subsidies. A.L.14.

1. What was a subsidy?
2. How was it collected?
3. Who had to pay?
4. Copy the entry for Amberley in 1327.
5. Note any interesting points about names, numbers in the list and so on.
   W. Hudson ed., *Sussex Subsidies, 1296, 1327, 1332* (Sussex Record Society, vol. x).

Protestation Returns. A.L.15.

1. What were the Protestation Returns?
2. Copy out the entry for Amberley.
   R. G. Rice ed., *West Sussex Protestation Returns, 1641-1642* (Sussex Record Society, vol. v).

Directories. A.L.16.

1. What picture do you get of Amberley from the *Directories* of 1852 and 1938?
2. Summarise the entries, copying significant extracts.
3. What important changes took place between 1852 and 1938? Note their causes and effects, if you can.
   Kelly, *Directories of Sussex*, 1852 and 1938.

Population. A.L.17.

1. Construct a population graph for Amberley, 1801-1901.
2. What information about the population can you get from the 1961 Census Returns?

Victoria County History, Sussex, vol. ii, pp. 215-28.
1961 Census Returns.

Custumal. A.L.18.

1. What was a custumal?
2. When was Amberley custumal compiled?
3. What points of interest emerge from it?
4. Copy the first twelve lines of the first page.

W. D. Peckham ed., *Custumals of the Sussex Manors of the Bishop of Chichester* (Sussex Record Society, vol. xxxi).

Agriculture since the late Eighteenth Century. A.L.19.

1. What can you discover about agricultural changes which have taken place in the Amberley district since 1750?
2. From the 1 in. to 1 ml. Land Utilisation Map of the 1930's, make a coloured land use map of Amberley parish on the scale of 2½ ins. to 1 ml.: use a duplicated sketch map and the same system of colouring as used on the 1 in. map.

Victoria County History of Sussex, vol. ii, pp. 273-90.
A. Young, *General View of the Agriculture . . . of Sussex* (Board of Agriculture Report, 2nd ed., 1808).
A. Briault, *Sussex* (Land Utilisation Survey Report, 1942) and L.U.S. Map, Sheet 133.
R. H. B. Jesse, *A Survey of the Agriculture of Sussex* (Royal Agricultural Society of England, 1960).
G. E. Fussell, 'Four Centuries of Farming Systems in Sussex', *Sussex Archaeological Collections*, vol. xc.
H. C. K. Henderson, 'The 1801 Crop Returns for Sussex', *Sussex Archaeological Collections*, vol. xc.

Enclosure. A.L.20.

1. What was Parliamentary Enclosure?
2. When was Amberley enclosed?

W. E. Tate, 'Sussex Enclosures', *Sussex Archaeological Collections*, vol. lxxxviii.

The Southdown Sheep. A.L.21.

1. What are the chief characteristics of the Southdown sheep?
2. What was the importance of John Ellman?

E. W. Lloyd, *The Southdown Sheep* (Chichester, Southdown Sheep Society, 1936).
Annals of Agriculture, vol. 11, p. 345 and vol. 20, p. 172.
Dictionary of National Biography.
M. A. Lower, *The Worthies of Sussex* (Lewes, Bacon, 1865).

Village Administration. A.L.22.

Summarise the section on village administration in Bonham-Carter, *The English Village*, pp. 139-60.
V. Bonham-Carter, *The English Village* (Penguin Books, 1952).

The General Development of English Village Life and Agriculture. A.L.23.

1. Summarise the account of the development of English farming and village life given in Bonham-Carter, *The English Village*, pp. 15-97.
2. Into what three periods could you divide this development?

V. Bonham-Carter, *The English Village* (Penguin Books, 1952).

(b) Local History in College of Education General Lecture Courses.

The following are samples from, and not comprehensive accounts of, local history work in individual colleges.

(i) Portsmouth: History (Main Course). Dr. M. J. Sydenham and Colleagues.

During the first year of the course a strong emphasis is placed on local history. We aim to show the students the educational and academic value of environmental work, introduce them to some of the principal sources available in libraries and record offices, and teach them to recognise different architectural styles. This is achieved primarily by group investigation of a local history topic during one term, for example, late medieval Southampton, Southwick village, the development of Portsmouth. Throughout the remainder of the course local history is introduced wherever appropriate, and frequent visits are made to places of historic interest in the neighbourhood.

(ii) Weymouth : History (Main Course). Miss M. B. Weinstock.

Second year students have a short lecture-discussion course (usually six meetings) on each of three sources of local history —architecture, heraldry and documents. The nature and content of the sources are considered, and so is their relevance to teaching. All documentary examples relate to Dorset, as do most, but not all, of the architectural and heraldic illustrations. We hope that, having attended the courses, students will be able to recognise the main features of domestic and ecclesiastical architecture and to interpret heraldic devices, and that they will use these kinds of material in school. The documents studied are taken mainly from parish chests. All students handle the real thing, but, of course, not all learn to read them. Apart from enabling them all to see some primary sources of written information, the aim is to encourage keen students to develop their interest in this field and to discourage others from attempting to use material for which they are not properly equipped, and thus to save local archivists from stupid enquiries.

(iii) Winchester: History (Curriculum Course).
Mr. E. B. Shipley and Colleagues.

This course for non-specialist history teachers lasts one year and contains a strong element of local history. We illustrate some of the main features of national history through the history of Winchester, in lectures and by visits. We join with the Art and Craft Department to run a well-attended optional course of lectures on various aspects of architecture (for example, churches, houses, building materials, clay and its products, furniture), illustrated with slides of Winchester subjects. We deliberately restrict ourselves to Winchester in order to show the students what a wealth of material lies at their door. All members of the course visit, under our guidance, during the year, a prehistoric site, a church, a cathedral, a castle and a country-house, and discuss their history and the teaching possibilities which they afford. As far as possible, the students take an active part in the planning and follow up work. Recently, for the first time, some students have also undertaken a group study of a Winchester suburb, Weeke. This introduced them, in a practical way, to the types of sources, methods of work and techniques of presentation involved, and gave many of them the confidence to attempt such work in school.

(c) University of Southampton Institute of Education.

Mr. R. Douch.

Individual Studies.

The studies described were written by students following the Third Year Supplementary Course in History at the City of Portsmouth College of Education, the Art Teacher's Diploma Course at the Bournemouth and Poole College of Art, and the part-time Diploma in Education course of this Institute.

Many of the subjects which can be usefully studied can be broadly classified according to the main type of source material on which they are based. Printed records are often neglected: 'Public Health in Late Medieval Southampton' was based on published borough records, 'The Extension of the Southampton Borough Boundary in 1920' on printed Council Minutes and newspapers. The latter offer endless opportunities: 'The Hampshire Telegraph, June-December, 1805', for instance, analysed the news and advertisements and related them to the general history of the time, while 'The Swing Riots in Hampshire' derived most of its material from published reports of disturbances and the trial of the rioters. Essay topics based on unpublished documents have included, for example, 'The Relief of Poverty in the Parish of St. Swithun, Winchester, 1600-1750', (overseers' accounts, settlement certificates and apprenticeship indentures); 'The Peartree National School, Southampton, 1869-1881', (log books, correspondence and accounts); and 'The Portsmouth Lunatic Asylum in 1896', (Council Minutes and papers).

Relatively few essays, such as 'Clay Tobacco Pipes from Portsmouth Excavations', have utilised excavated archaeological remains, but field archaeology and architecture have given rise to a large number which have often been illustrated with original photographs and drawings. These have included conventional architectural-historical studies like 'Christchurch Castle' and 'Church Memorials in South Dorset', but more usually topics such as 'Ryde Pier', 'Bournemouth Shop Fronts' and 'Purbeck Stone in Swanage' have been encouraged.

Good essays involving the use of a greater variety of sources have concerned, for example, 'Land Use in a Sussex Parish in the Nineteenth and Twentieth Centuries', 'The Rise of the Worthing Tomato Industry', 'The Story of a Street: Throop Road, Bournemouth', and 'The Growth of a Southampton Suburb: Woolston'. The examples quoted by no means exhaust the variety of types of subject on which individual studies in local history may be based.

Several important lessons have been learned from extensive experience of supervising and examining such studies. It is essential for the tutor to decide what is the purpose of the essay. While it may sometimes constitute an exercise in the collection of teaching material, it will more usually represent an introduction to historical method, involving the collection, assessment, selection and presentation of information. The distinction is of the utmost importance since the former is likely to result in a purely descriptive piece of writing, while the latter should entail critical and analytical evaluation. Considerable help should be given to students in enabling them to choose suitable topics: their initial interests are important, but they can be over-emphasised. The availability of suitable material is an important factor to consider at an early stage. The detailed treatment of a limited subject is preferable to a wide-ranging superficial survey. It is possible to lay too much stress on the use of original documents: printed sources offer many opportunities, and a fresh approach to familiar materials can often be as rewarding as conventional work on new sources.

Profitable local work is not an easy option and, when topics are selected from this field, there is much to be said in favour of their being related to the College neighbourhood since the tutor is then in a position to give students more help. Maximum benefit is unlikely to be derived from any study unless there is careful tutorial supervision throughout.[1]

(d) Bournemouth and Poole College of Art. Mr. R. Douch.

Individual Studies based on Aspects of a Single Settlement.

Twenty students working for the Art Teacher's Diploma.

The chief aims of this project were to interest the students in the history of local communities, especially in the visible remains of their history; to show them how to discover relevant material relating to it, much of which would be useful to them as teachers of art, craft and general subjects; and to provide each with a topic for an individual study which he had to write as part of his course. Formerly these essay subjects had been chosen independently and were concerned with local history in any part of the country.

The students did most of the work in their own time. Three introductory talks on sources and techniques were given and a group visit was made to the settlement chosen for study.

This settlement, easily accessible from Bournemouth, was Wimborne, a market town in Dorset which the tutor knew well. Topics suggested as suitable included: settlement site and pattern; place names; geology and geography; local maps; agriculture; industry; shops and services; markets; communications (rivers, roads, bridges, railways); building surveys; churches; chapels; almshouses; country houses; schools; minor

[1]See also R. Douch and F. W. Steer, *Local History Essays: Some Notes for Students* (University of Southampton, Institute of Education, 1960).

domestic architecture; architectural detail; archaeological remains; and a limited chronological period in the history of the town. It was stressed that present day aspects, with their historical background, (for example, building; good and bad planning; the work of local government; recreation) could be as acceptable as more obviously historical topics. Essays were to be illustrated by the students' own drawings and photographs.

Topics were then freely chosen. There was some overlap and eventually essays were submitted on the following subjects: The Physical Background; Badbury Rings, an Iron Age Hill-fort; The Building Materials of Wimborne; History revealed in Architecture; Georgian Architecture; The Medieval History of the Church of Wimborne Minster; Church Monuments and Memorials; St. Margaret's Chapel and Almshouses; Queen Elizabeth's Grammar School; Kingston Lacy House, (a) The Exterior, (b) The Interior; The Mill on the Stour; Manor Farm, Hampreston; The Market; Dorset Roads; and The Wimborne to Dorchester Railway.

The scheme worked well. At first, one or two students were disappointed that they were not given absolute freedom to choose their essay topic, but this feeling soon disappeared. By studying a topic in the neighbourhood students found that they could work on their essays more continuously throughout the year, and their concentrating on a single settlement resulted in considerable interchange of ideas. Tutorial supervision was also easier and more effective. A theme in national or local history could equally well form the common element in work of this nature, and either could be made the basis, if so desired, of a comprehensive discussion of sources.

(e) City of Portsmouth College of Education. Mr. J. G. Webb.

Introduction to Palaeography.

Supplementary History Course students: each year.

The study of palaeography. It has been developed not only in the belief that familiarity with original records adds a new dimension to historical understanding and fosters a more critical and realistic approach to source material, but also in the hope that those who thereby have overcome the initial difficulties involved in learning to read a variety of English hands will be encouraged to attempt original research, if only of a limited character, on some aspects of the historical development of their own localities. Moreover a knowledge of palaeography helps those teachers who wish to introduce their pupils to photographic copies of historical documents. It is also firmly believed that others, engaged in teaching young children to read, will have a better understanding of the problems involved, if they themselves, at a mature age, have consciously experienced a similar kind of learning process.

About one hour a week for a term is sufficient to give students a good basic working knowledge.

Initially students work from Hilda Grieve's *Examples of English Handwriting* and progress to photostats and microfilm of documents from both local and national archives. These include parish and town records, business accounts, wills, inventories, state papers, correspondence, extracts from an early nineteenth century diary, and a naval logbook. The characteristics of each class of document are discussed.

Medieval documents are not normally included because most of the students do not have a good working knowledge of Latin. They often come to college under the misapprehension that all research on original records before *c.*1700 is barred to them, and I try to show them that in fact a great deal of material in English is available. Having gained a grounding in a variety of English hands, the more enthusiastic and those with Latin are able to extend their range after further practice with little outside help. As soon as the group as a whole has reached a reasonable standard of proficiency, I move on to a specific piece of editing.

The students are very enthusiastic about the subject and many of them say that they will make use of their knowledge at a later date, but it is difficult to know how many do.

(f) City of Portsmouth College of Education. Mr. J. G. Webb.

Editing Local Documents.

Supplementary History Course students: each year.

This work familiarises students with particular kinds of records and with techniques of editing. It also makes a contribution to the study of the history of Portsmouth.

About a term is devoted to the project. The students meet once a week for approximately an hour and a half. At first we use the time for transcribing, but once initial problems have been resolved, copying is done by the students in their own time, and official periods are occupied by discussions in which editorial principles are established and the significance of the document and its background are examined in detail.

The task and the problems of the editor are fully discussed and, each year, an attempt is made to transcribe, edit and study a self-contained group of records. The documents come from both local and national archives. Sometimes we work on original records, sometimes from photostats. Every student's transcript is checked by a fellow-student (and by me!). Three volumes in the College Record Series have been completed:

1. 'From Portsmouth to West Africa, 1553-54: the Wills of the Mariners of the *Primrose*'. The thirty wills which make up the text are valuable for the new light that they throw on Thomas Wyndham's last voyage.
2. 'Portsmouth Apprenticeship Indentures, 1594-1648'. All the known enrolled indentures for the period were examined and analysed, and a group of interesting examples edited.
3. 'A Survey of the Defences of the Town and Harbour of Portsmouth, 1745'. This makes available for the first time a clear and accurate picture of the town's defences at a particularly interesting period.

Each completed text, with its introduction, appendices,

maps and tables, is bound and placed in the College Library for use by future students.

If the work is to be done in a scholarly and professional way, a lot of responsibility and hard work falls on the tutor. He has to instil the need for absolute accuracy and care, which is more difficult than it may seem, and keep the editing under close scrutiny.

(g) King Alfred's College, Winchester.

Mr. E. B. Shipley and Colleagues.

Informal Local History Activities.

(i) All main-course History students undertake a spare-time extra which they pursue under general supervision. At present these groups are engaged in prehistoric field work (the systematic investigation of unploughed downland in Hampshire); palaeography (the study of sixteenth century borough records); vernacular architecture (including the making of measured plans); and 'digging' (on a variety of sites in Southampton). These activities are inspired and loosely directed by the staff, but no written work has to be submitted. The students begin work in their first year, and it is hoped that they will continue to take an active interest throughout their course. Naturally, as long as the amount achieved is left to the individual, some will do more work than others. But this is probably as it should be.

(ii) In the past two years three long week-ends in different parts of the country (Cheltenham, Sussex and Worcester) have been arranged for main historians, approximately twenty-five students taking part in each. They consist of visits by coach and on foot to places of interest, avoiding many of the standard sites. Their purpose is both social and historical. The historical aim is to show the characteristics and potential of different areas, and to visit places mentioned in College teaching which are inaccessible on day trips. So far these weekends have been optional, but they are likely to become a regular feature with compulsory attendance at at least one during each student's course. When this happens, the students will be encouraged to take a greater part in arranging the visits which will also be more closely integrated with their general course work than they are at present.

(iii) Coach visits are arranged each term, one or two in the autumn and spring, three or four in the summer. The programme is varied and often unusual, the aim being to encourage students to go to less popular and out of the way places that are worth seeing.

(iv) The History Society organises regular walks on Sundays throughout the year. These vary between five and fifteen miles, depending on the time of year and the nature of the terrain, and take in features of historical interest, such as barrows, churches, houses, deserted villages, battlefields and disused railways. One of the staff usually does the talking, though occasionally a member of the student committee describes a site.

(v) Schemes are afoot to start some more active local history for members of the History Society. Archaeological excavation, brass-rubbing, and a photographic competition have been suggested. All would be based on the College neighbourhood.

(h) University of Southampton Institute of Education.

Mr. R. Douch.

An Outline Plan and Reading Scheme on the History of a County.

Practising teachers, following the part-time course leading to the award of the Diploma in Education and choosing History as a main subject, undertake this type of work.

Few members of these groups are history specialists and the object is to introduce them to some of the most valuable books and articles on local history, and to enable them to gather relevant and accurate material useful to themselves, and the children they teach, with as little waste of time and effort as possible. While much of the material would be useful in studying the history of local communities, this particular exercise is primarily intended to provide local illustrations for use in general history teaching.

The work is spread over the first year of the three-year course.

Note-making and the drawing of maps and diagrams on the basis of carefully directed reading are the essential features of the scheme. The work is divided into seventeen sections as follows: General Works, The Geological and Geographical Background, Maps, Prehistoric Hampshire, Romano-British Hampshire, Saxon Hampshire, Agriculture, Industry, Transport and Communications, Architecture, Divisions and Administration, Towns and Villages, The New Forest, The Isle of Wight, Hampshire in National History, Famous Hampshire Men and Women, and Local Museums. It is suggested that examples to illustrate general points should be taken, where possible and desirable, from the locality in which the student teaches.

The instructions for three sections are included here.

6. Saxon Hampshire.

   Points to be covered should include:

   (i) notes on the conquest and settlement by the Saxons, their conversion to Christianity, their social and economic life, raids by Norsemen and conquest by the Normans.

   (ii) the kingdom of Wessex.

   (iii) Hampshire place names.

   (iv) list of churches in Hampshire showing Saxon work.

   (v) translation, with commentary, of a local entry in Domesday Book.

Make your notes from:

D. Whitelock, *The Beginning of English Society* (Penguin Books, 1952).

B. Carpenter Turner, *A History of Hampshire* (Darwen Finlayson, 1963).

E. Ekwall, *The Concise Oxford Dictionary of English Place Names* (4th ed., Oxford, Clarendon Press, 1960).

A. R. and P. M. Green, *Saxon Architecture and Sculpture in Hampshire* (Winchester, Warren, 1951).

H. C. Darby and E. M. C. Campbell, *The Domesday Geography of South-East England* (Cambridge University Press, 1962).

Victoria County History, Hampshire, vol. i, pp. 399-526, 'Domesday Survey'.

9. Transport and Communications.
   (i) Draw maps of Hampshire showing the roads included in the Ordnance Survey, *Map of Roman Britain* (3rd ed., 1956) and the Ordnance Survey, *Map of England in the Seventeenth Century* (1930): comment briefly on their distribution.
   (ii) Find examples of markets and fairs formerly held in your part of Hampshire: note their duration and importance. Make notes on St. Giles Fair, Winchester. See W. White, *History, Gazetteer and Directory of Hampshire* (Sheffield, 1859) and B. Vesey-Fitzgerald, 'Hampshire Fairs', *Hampshire Review*, vol. xii, pp. 8-13.
   (iii) From C. Hadfield, *The Canals of Southern England* (Phoenix House, 1955), write brief notes on Hampshire canals.
   (iv) Summarise briefly the development of the railway system in Hampshire: see C. F. D. Marshall, *History of the Southern Railway*, 2 vols. (2nd ed., I. Allan, 1963).

16. Famous Men and Women.
   Make a list of important persons and families born in, or connected with, the county. Indicate the places with which they were connected and, where necessary, mention why these people were important. See J. C. Cox, rev. R. L. P. Jowitt, *Hampshire* (7th ed., Methuen, 1949) and K. E. Innes, *Hampshire Pilgrimages: Men and Women who have sojourned in Hampshire* (London, W. Sessions, 1948).

Teachers always comment on the value of this directed reading and start to use some of the material in their lessons long before they have completed the scheme.

(i) City of Portsmouth College of Education. Mr. J. G. Webb.

A History Teaching Unit: The Visit of the Allied Sovereigns to Portsmouth in 1814.

The group consisted of twelve practising teachers attending an evening course.

The aim was to produce, from reliable primary and secondary sources, an authoritative and comprehensive teaching unit as the first of a series to help the busy classroom teacher.

Eight weekly meetings were held. The early ones took the form of lecture-discussions on sources and, as the teachers developed their studies in their own time, later meetings consisted of progress reports and tutorials.

Each teacher worked, under guidance, on a particular aspect of the Allied Sovereigns' visit to the city from 22nd-25th June, 1814. Napoleon had been banished to Elba and the royal visitors to England were given the opportunity of seeing the navy in its real home, Portsmouth. Amongst the sources used in an attempt to reconstruct the occasion were standard general histories and biographies; histories, guide-books and directories of Portsmouth, newspapers and journals; printed memoirs, diaries and letters; maps; and manuscripts, both national and local.

The completed Unit includes historical information and teaching aids. Thus there is a file of notes on aspects of the national and local background and on details of the visit itself, such as the reasons and preparations for it, the condition of the town, the decorations, the state dinners, the visit to the dockyard and the review of the fleet. There is also a collection of illustrations and photostat copies of documents which were carefully chosen to encourage active exploration of relevant themes by the children. With this material, the 1814 visit could be taught for its own sake or as part of a general course. Teachers in both primary and secondary schools should be able to select features suited to their particular needs. It is hoped to make the Unit available to teachers through the city's School Loans Service.

(ii) JUNIOR SCHOOLS

(a) St. John's Junior Mixed School, Southampton. Mr. E. T. Oxborrow.

Southampton in Saxon and Medieval Times.

Class 1 : 40 boys and girls, aged 9 to 11 : full range of ability.

This work replaced formal history lessons in part of a chronological course on British History from 1714 to the present day.

It occupied one hour per week of History time and occasionally Art and Craft periods throughout one term. Visits were made after school and on Saturday mornings.

St. John's is situated within the town's medieval walls, a stone's throw from the water, in the heart of down-town Southampton. In 1962, when the school buildings were being extended, a stone structure was discovered beneath the playground. This fascinated many of the older children who were eager to examine it and to find out all they could about its age and purpose. The museum staff identified our 'find' as a medieval wine vault. Spontaneously, we started to delve into the history of the town.

During the year we investigated various aspects of local history, but we spent most time on Saxon and Medieval Southampton, remains from which lay close at hand, both above and below ground. I knew very little about this topic when we began, but books, pamphlets, maps, photographs and excavated remains, in the public library and museum, soon enabled me to establish the broad outlines of developments and to know where we might discover particular details. We visited other vaults and some of the important medieval buildings, such as the Bargate and God's House Tower. We also traced the line of the town walls, and appreciated how small an area they enclosed. We learnt about the importance of the medieval port both for trade and in war. The advantages of the raised ground on which medieval Southampton grew were compared with the low-lying sites of the earlier Roman and Saxon settlements. The children, working in groups, drew maps and plans, made notes and drawings, and constructed scale models, using balsa wood and papier-maché, of the Saxon and medieval towns. These models were very detailed and included figures and boats. The children greatly enjoyed building them and took great pains to ensure their accuracy.

The initial interest in discoveries beneath the surface was maintained. Groups of boys and girls sat on the playground wall watching the borough archaeologist excavate adjacent sites. And, almost daily, assorted 'finds' were brought to school, mostly pottery and clay pipes, but once a cannon ball. I was puzzled to know where the children found all these until I discovered that they had persuaded labourers working nearby on the construction of a new road to collect material for them!

On another occasion, I should make more use of illustrations, both transparencies of present buildings and old prints, and I should talk less during visits. Certain aspects, such as the trade of the town, could also be developed by using extracts from the city archives, many of which are published and translated. No major problems were encountered. There was something which everyone, whatever his ability, could do, and the children were immensely interested. Their search for information, which necessitated a good supply of general and local history books, led to the establishment of the now flourishing school library. Undoubtedly, this was the most successful year's work in history that I have experienced in twenty years' teaching in junior schools.

(b) Western C. of E. Primary School, Winchester.

Mr. J. A. Gunner.

Visit to the Westgate Museum, Winchester.

Fourth year class: 47 boys and girls, aged 10-11 years: mixed ability.

The visit formed part of a wider scheme, 'Know your City', undertaken during the children's last term and a half in the junior school. I wanted them to study the Westgate as a building, to understand its original function as a gateway to the medieval city, and to identify and appreciate a small number of museum exhibits.

Thirty minutes were spent at the Museum. The total time given to preparation, visit and follow-up by each child was usually about seven or eight hours, occasionally more.

Before the visit the children brought old postcards, books, pictures and verbal snippets pertaining to the Westgate. These were discussed and an idea of what to look for, and where, was obtained. A day or two before the visit the children were given a broadsheet containing both information and questions. We went through this, and a few questions were answered before the visit. At the Westgate, the class divided into two groups. One, with a student in charge, went to view the Great Hall of the nearby Castle; the other remained with me. The groups spent half an hour in each place. The exterior of the Westgate was examined first, attention being drawn to features such as the windows on the east, but not on the west, side, and the portcullis grooves. The children were asked to volunteer any information they knew or, where desirable, to have a reasonable guess.

Once inside the Museum, I reminded the children of the main exhibits which they had to find and study. These included the set of early Tudor weights and measures, two executioner's axes, and small collections of armour and domestic utensils. Then followed a short period of directed searching and studying, after which the children were given time for individual browsing, sketching and note-making. The last five minutes were devoted to ensuring that the main tasks had been completed. Most children, with the exception of those of limited ability, had done quite well. They used rough notebooks to record any information, sketch or rubbing, and these, plus their broadsheets, were to provide the basis for later work.

Most children recorded the results of their visit in individual booklets, but a minority worked in pairs. These booklets contained written work, drawings, sketches, postcards and rubbings of inscriptions on the walls. Large paintings were displayed separately. The visit also produced some useful oral work. The children described and discussed the most interesting and the most surprising things which they had seen. A short question-time, designed to clear up outstanding points, followed, when most of the questions asked by individual children were answered by other members of the class. Finally, the answers to the questions on the broadsheet were checked.

The value of the visit and the subsequent work was best judged by the children's reactions. The very act of leaving the classroom and going into the outside world helped to correct the erroneous notion that the two are separate entities. Although the Westgate was a familiar building, only a few of the children had previously been inside it. The realisation that it had served an important utilitarian purpose for the citizens of the medieval city came as a shock, and an inanimate lump of stone in their environment acquired a new significance. The visit also stimulated old, and created new, interests, and the resulting work was generally of a higher standard than usual.

On another such visit, I would arrange that the children worked in small groups during the time for browsing so that those of limited ability would have a more able child to help them. One problem that I found in the follow-up work was the children's inability to paraphrase from reference books. The number of text and reference books consulted, and the extent to which they were used, was impressive, but the results were too often a word-for-word copy. No doubt, intelligent note-making will follow with increasing practice and maturity.

(c) Storrington County Primary School, Sussex.

Parham House. Mr. R. A. Carter.

38 boys and girls, aged 10 to 11: A and B streams.

The primary object was to produce a model of Parham House, a magnificent Elizabethan mansion about three miles from the school. The work broadened to become a centre of inter-

> est around which much of the work of the class developed in history, geography, English, art, and even mathematics.

Approximately six hours a week for eight weeks were spent on this work.

The only special qualifications of the teacher were a love of modelling and enthusiasm. A considerable amount of preliminary preparation was necessary: in particular, as detailed a plan as possible of Parham House itself had to be obtained. This proved difficult since so many alterations and modifications have taken place over the centuries. Eventually, sufficient photographs and drawings were available for me to be able to draw up plans to a scale suitable for the children to use. Everything was then ready for work to begin.

The model was still the limited objective, but once a few of the more able boys had started work, others in the class showed increasing interest. To satisfy this interest more and more books and drawings became necessary. One thing led to another and we were able to appoint groups, each under a leader, to develop a particular line of enquiry. Some, mainly boys, proved to be the better 'artisans', and they were allocated the task of construction. At a later stage, when more detailed work, such as decorating, became necessary, girls took over from the boys.

The whole of the building, which measured about 2 ft. × 1 ft. 6 ins. × 8 ins., was in balsa wood. The windows were made from a plastic glass. For colouring, we mixed our own powder paints. The finished building was firmly fixed to a base of fibre board. This we found could be roughened sufficiently to give the effect of grass. A cut-out background, depicting the line of the downs and the trees surrounding Parham, was then placed behind the House. While this work was in progress, other groups drew items of particular interest, such as doorways, fireplaces, articles of clothing and furniture. Yet others were engaged in historical enquiries, and we were able eventually to produce a small booklet which we called 'A Brief History of Parham'. This booklet traced the development of Parham as an estate from just before the Norman Conquest to the present day: it included drawings and photographs taken from magazines and leaflets, and was bound by the children.

We were given great assistance in our search for information by the librarian at the local branch of the County Library. She happened to be the mother of one of the boys involved and came to our aid by unearthing a very old, but comprehensive, history of Parham. Much of our subsequent work was based on this since, apart from guide books, we found scarcely any other printed material that the children could use. We also visited the House itself, and obtained many items of interest from parents and grandparents. Many of these people had intimate knowledge of the estate through past connections as employees there.

When we had completed our task, everyone had an increased awareness of why Parham was there, a better knowledge of how communities, such as the one we live in, have developed, and a much more enquiring mind. The only difficulties encountered were those of numbers. The interest aroused was so great that, at times, it was difficult to deal adequately with all the queries that arose. When I undertake this kind of work again, I shall have a clearer plan before we begin and then pursue fewer lines of enquiry at any one time. The work will be tabulated under definite headings so that fewer groups will be necessary and less movement involved.

(d) The Desmond Anderson County Junior School,
Crawley, Sussex. Mr. F. Keenlyside.

Sussex in Maps.

The maps were made by 2nd, 3rd and 4th year children in mixed non-streamed classes.

The aims of this work were to interest the children, many of whom had moved from London to this new town, in their neighbourhood and in maps and map-making and to provide display material. Eight of the maps, mounted and framed, hang in the school, arouse considerable interest, and are used as teaching aids.

Possible topics were discussed at a staff meeting and class teachers chose the aspects on which their classes would work. Most were maps of Sussex, though some covered only the Crawley area. Several were mainly geographical: thus there was a 'Relief Map of Sussex' and maps of 'Sussex Rivers', 'Railways', 'Roads and Distances', and 'Woodlands around Ifield'. The 'Pictorial Map of Sussex', the needlework 'Map of Sussex', and 'The School Address in Maps' all included some historical information. Those most concerned with history were 'Rapes and Castles', 'Cavalier and Roundhead Houses', 'Turnpikes', 'Fields in Crawley 150 Years Ago', and 'Places to Visit'. Most of the maps measured approximately 20 ins. × 18 ins. With the exception of the needlework map, they were all painted, many being made by sticking individual items on to a base map.

The information used in making the maps was obtained from modern Ordnance Survey maps, books and periodicals relating to the county, and photostat copies of old maps which the school bought quite cheaply from the British Museum. These included part of Yeakell and Gardner's *Sussex* (1795); the 2 ins. to 1 ml. O.S. field drawing (1808) for the 1st ed. of the 1 in. to 1 ml. map of the Crawley district; and the 1st ed. of the local O.S. 6 ins. to 1 ml. map (1869-74).

A detailed account follows of the making of 'The Pictorial Map of Sussex'. This was the work of the second year class of 36 boys and girls under the guidance of their class-teacher, Mr. D. R. Rogers. Making the map took approximately three weeks, but research and the preparation of material for use by the children took the greater part of the previous term.

Relevant information collected from the sources described above was simplified into a series of topic books for the children to use which were classified under various headings, such as 'Sussex Customs', 'Transport' and 'Farming'. Where possible, these were written in story form and each page ended with a series of tasks for the children, involving written work and illustration. Each book was in loose-leaf form to facilitate both individual and group work. The children were encouraged to collect suitable material. This included old press cuttings, tourist brochures and picture postcards. A small class museum was also formed.

As interest grew, the time spent on this work increased and sometimes whole afternoons were devoted to it. The children were impatient to see the map completed and undertook additional work during playtimes, lunch hours and after school. The basic framework of the map, measuring five feet by four, was completed by a group of six children who obtained the necessary enlargement by the system of 'squaring off'. They were meticulous in their efforts to be accurate. Once the main outline was finished, they carefully marked in the towns, rivers, main roads and railways. As the children completed their notes and illustrations these were stuck into position, and they gave five-minute talks on their chosen topics.

The work had a purpose and aroused great interest and pride amongst the children. These continued in their later work, when many compiled their own maps and the class suggested that we should make a series called 'The School Address in Maps'. With second-year children, the main problem was the difficulty of obtaining information suited to their age. This was solved by the system of topic books, but these took a long time to prepare.

(e) Butlocks Heath County Primary School, Hampshire.

Mr. K. Roach.

History Around Us: a study, arising from references in two of the school log-books covering the period 1876-1927, of aspects of local and national life from Victorian times onwards.

4A: 36 boys and girls, aged 10-11 years.

The work was designed to correlate various subjects, mathematics, art and craft, and English, for example, as well as history. Thus, our activities included surveying the school building with homemade instruments; constructing graphs of statistics; making clay models to display costume and a cardboard model of the school; drawing; painting; and writing. The references in the log-books provided a real springboard for this correlation and for investigating the history of the school, the neighbourhood, and the nation.

The time taken for this work came from that allotted to History (1 hour a week for one term), Mathematics (2-3 hours a week for 6 weeks), and Art and Craft (about 6 hours per child spread over the term).

The project was introduced by a talk about the log-books: individual cards, giving quotations and made beforehand, were described, and some were read out. Then the children listened to a tape-recorded history of the school, made by the headmaster for another purpose, and noted interesting facts. Individuals and pairs chose a topic from the log-books, the cards, or their notes in order to write one or more illustrated articles for the class book, 'History Around Us'. This eventually contained thirty-three chapters. All of these utilised log-book material, some more than others. Among the former were topics such as the history of the school (founded in 1876), subjects studied, holidays (official and unofficial), attendance figures, infectious diseases (there were outbreaks of diphtheria, small-pox and scarlet fever in the area in the 1870's and 1880's), and local dignitaries (many of whom visited the school). Some of the chapters which derived less of their information from the log-books themselves, such as the parish of Hound in the nineteenth century and the story of Netley Abbey, concerned the neighbourhood. Others described aspects of national history which had a local connection—biographies of David Livingstone and Captain Scott (both mentioned in the log-books), Victorian houses, clothes and transport (one of the local people rode in a brougham), and the famous military hospital, the Royal Victoria Hospital, built at Netley after the Crimean War. Whenever possible, past conditions were compared with the present.

Reference books were borrowed from the school and public libraries: the teacher and children brought others from home. The class visited Netley Hospital, Netley Abbey and Hound Church. Groups of children interviewed the Vicar of Netley and old inhabitants. The articles were written as rough proofs and were corrected by other children and/or the teacher. They were then written up on one side of standard size paper and stuck on leaves of sugar paper. The resulting large volume was bound in card covered with wallpaper. Every child read the book, commented on it and questioned the writers of individual articles.

The work was extremely valuable because the range of topics allowed individual interests to be fully exploited. The relationship between the history of the school, the locality, and national events and personalities was clearly seen and grew naturally from the common bond of references in the log-books. The reports on visits and interviews gave confidence to the reporters and were instructive and entertaining to the rest of the class. The individual cards were invaluable. A large supply of reference books was needed and obtained: nevertheless the book supply had to be carefully organised because, on many occasions, different children were eager to consult the same volumes.

(f) Highbury Junior Mixed and Infants School, Cosham, Portsmouth. — Mr. L. Law and Mr. W. Holleyoak.

A Study of the Village of Southwick.

Fourth year junior class: 47 boys and girls: mixed ability.

Our introduction to this type of work came from a BBC broadcast to schools and the children found it so enjoyable that it has become a regular feature of the syllabus. It takes the place of History, Geography and English Composition lessons. Southwick, about four miles from the school, is the nearest village to Portsmouth.

On average, three hours a week for one year were devoted to this work in class: in addition five visits to the village were made by the whole class and many by smaller groups to study particular topics.

The work consisted of a study of many aspects—historical,

geographical and sociological—of the village. The teachers involved spent a considerable time in local libraries and three days in the Hampshire County Record Office at Winchester gathering material and preparing the content of the work. Many sources were used. The aim was always to go to as authentic a source as possible. Historical sources included Domesday Book; the charters of Southwick Priory; Godwin's *Civil War in Hampshire*; Carlyle's, *Letters of Oliver Cromwell*; the will of Richard Norton, 1713; the schedules completed by the village in 1804 when invasion threatened; copies of the *Hampshire Telegraph* for 1803-4; Ordnance Survey maps since 1910; estate records for 1813; the minute book of the Fareham Union workhouse, 1835; the log book of Southwick Primary School; the *Proceedings of the Hampshire Field Club*; and Chester Wilmot's *The Invasion of Europe*. Most of these, or extracts from them, were used by the children.

Besides consulting written sources, the children made as many visits as possible. Often they split up into various groups to specialise in one particular aspect. For example, when the class visited *H.M.S. Dryad*, which occupies Southwick House and was the headquarters of General Eisenhower immediately before 'D Day', groups of children specialised as follows: the grounds; the external architecture of the house; the map of 'D day' naval positions; the room where the meetings were held; and interior architecture. Visits were also made to the site of a motte and bailey castle, a farm, the school, the church, a Parish Council meeting, Easter Sunday service, and the Southwick Estate manager's office. Clinometer measurements were made of parts of the church, and a small section of the Roman road, which runs through the parish, was uncovered. A farming survey was carried out by submitting a form to local farmers: eighteen out of twenty-two completed and returned it. A traffic census was organised and the types of buildings in the village were studied. The children's recording consisted mainly of written work and drawings arising from their visits or from material presented to them. Some of this was later written up and illustrated as a class study in a loose-leaf book.

Experience shows that the children become very interested

and often make their own visits to study a particular feature. The work is alive and real, and its scope is wide enough for every child, whatever his intelligence, to find something useful to undertake. Such work also increases the children's general interest in the countryside around them.

(g) Ifield County Junior School, Crawley, Sussex. Headmaster: Mr. A. Worthy.

The Changing Face of Crawley.

The whole school took part. We sometimes explore a theme throughout the school so that when the work is put together the close relationship between different aspects can be enjoyed by all. Such a theme presented itself in 1964 when Crawley reached a certain stage of maturity with the completion of its Civic Buildings and other major projects. Some five hundred boys and girls of very varying abilities were involved.

The aim of the work was to show how major developments in our environment come about through the efforts of many people, and to break down the 'they' concept. This is as much history as is the building of Norman castles.

The work occupied most of the summer term, but was interrupted by other activities. Both children and staff were well qualified to tackle such investigations by virtue of a long apprenticeship in 'discovery' methods. It would be a grave mistake to think that children can just be turned loose on a project such as this. A great deal of patient preparation has to be done first, such as finding out which people can help with their memories, photographs and records, and verbal accounts.

The topics studied were: *4th Year,* Hospital Development, The Work of Crawley Urban District Council, The Growth of Industry, Railway Development; *3rd Year,* Houses and Building, The Shrinking Countryside, The Post Office and its Changing Work; *2nd Year,* The Brighton Road, Farmers and their Farms; *1st Year,* The George Hotel as a Coaching Inn, Recreational Activities in Crawley, The Fire Service, Gatwick Airport and Aeroplanes.

More detailed descriptions are given of three of these projects.

Hospital Development. Mr. J. Albery.

A group of talented children produced a lively review of the growth of hospital facilities in the town, starting with the pioneer work of Sarah Robinson in 1896, when the first hospital was built. Such subjects as nurses' training and uniform and hospital conditions throughout the period were examined, and many of the benefits of medical research became apparent. Generous help from the matron and her staff enabled the children to study present day techniques. A group of boys found out about great physicians throughout history and studied the planning and building of the town's hospitals over seventy years. A review followed of the social implications from the days of voluntary hospitals to the facilities provided under the National Health Service.

The Work of the Crawley Urban District Council.
Mr. R. Buglass.

This class paid visits to the sewage works, the new swimming pool (where chlorination and filtration methods were studied), and to the nurseries of the Parks and Gardens Department. The work of refuse disposal, street cleansing, highway maintenance, and the planting of open spaces were presented in an interesting manner by the chief officers concerned, and a visit from the Treasurer showed how rates were calculated, collected and spent. One group studied the local elections, how they were conducted, the meaning of democracy, and the aspirations of the various contestants. A visit from a councillor gave the children a completely new idea of the day to day work of the Council members.

Houses and Building. Mrs. D. Wragg.

This group of ten-year-old children has lived through a period when some sixteen thousand houses have been, and are still being, built around them. The study of medieval houses may seem remote from their lives, but, when they have talked to builders and seen the techniques employed in present day building, the work of ancient craftsmen takes on a new significance. They watched bricklayers, carpenters, plasterers and painters in action, and talked with them. They compared Victorian and Edwardian with modern houses, and they studied the layout of industrial and shopping estates and the planning of their own village of Ifield. As a piece of recreational work at home, they made models of their own houses based on their own surveying and measurement. They also enjoyed talks by older residents who described, in considerable detail, living conditions in the houses, shops, fields, factories and hospital of the old town.

A wide variety of means of recording was employed, with an eye partly on a public exhibition where each class could enjoy the work of others and where those outside people who had helped us could see the tangible results of the investigation. Many models were made, showing, for example, the shrinking countryside. Diagrams and charts were valuable in the project on the hospital, indicating clearly daily timetables, menus and routine. The work on the 'George Hotel' lent itself to the writing of original poetry on themes such as coaching and the highwayman. By mounting the written work on standard sized sheets it was possible to assemble the material in book form when the exhibition was over, so that future children could profit from the discoveries made.

Certain difficulties are encountered in work on the recent past. By its very nature, little information is available in books. There is a small and decreasing body of people who have lived in the same place for fifty years or more. Some are extremely helpful with shrewd insight into changes which have taken place and a happy contact with children. The contributions of others need to be edited; and others yet again are more valuable for photographic and documentary records which they can lend. Knowledgeable people, such as councillors and factory managers, who in their work are shaping the modern world, must not be overtaxed.

I make no apology for calling all this local history. Perhaps as a profession teachers have tended to minimise what is familiar and under their noses in favour of what is rather sentimental and remote.

(h) Newlands Junior Mixed School, Southampton.
Mr. J. G. Espezel.

Get to Know Southampton: an Illustrated Notebook.

Fourth year children: approximately 90 boys and girls, aged 10-11 years: A to C range.

The aim was to encourage the children to learn more about their environment and, where possible, to form a link between local and national history. The notebook, which I planned and duplicated in colour, described some historical features of the city and provided opportunities for the children to record their own findings when visiting them. The field work was largely an out of school activity: discussion and further investigation took place in school.

The notebooks were completed in about six weeks, mainly at week-ends, but follow-up went on throughout the whole of the summer term.

The idea of making the notebook came to me when on holiday. My own children derived much pleasure from the 'I Spy' booklet, *On the Seashore*, and I realised that this scheme could be adapted for use in a local study which I was planning for the following year. My own interest was sharpened by the amount of research and verification which I had to undertake.

My object was to provide, for each topic, a certain amount of information to create interest and some questions for the children to answer. I hoped that, as they sought these answers, much useful incidental learning would take place. Above all, I wanted them to enjoy themselves and develop a liking for the subject. Cartoon drawings enlivened the pages and sketches of historical buildings and remains were included. The questions asked about topics all required personal observation or enquiry. Points were awarded according to difficulty or to the research required. Some pages were left blank for the children to use for additional information or sketches. They were encouraged to colour the printed sketches.

Weekly discussions were held and help was given to pupils requiring it. The children were very enthusiastic. Many parents co-operated and one told me that he had thoroughly enjoyed the experience as, despite thirty years' residence in the city, he had never before visited any of the historic buildings. Museum staff were most helpful to the children. Several models, individual booklets and other records were made, and a small exhibition of results was held. A prize was awarded to the pupil who completed the most interesting and original notebook.

I felt that the project was successful and that all the aims were achieved. The same type of booklet could be used in connection with visits to individual buildings of interest and museums.

(iii) SECONDARY SCHOOLS

(a) Lord Digby's School, Sherborne, Dorset. Miss B. Rose.

Pre-Roman Dorset.

First year: 26 girls: unstreamed.

The subject formed a natural introduction to a conventional, chronological grammar school syllabus on English history. I hoped to increase the children's awareness of history all around them and more specifically, to enable them to recognise certain types of prehistoric field remains. I also wanted to balance the 'story' aspect of history with a more scientific approach by narrowing the children's rather romantic vision of 'cave-men and hunters' to a limited period of prehistory in a limited area.

About 1½ hours a week, including homework, for four weeks were spent on this work, plus a single full day's visit.

Most of the work was done by formal class teaching: personal records were kept by each girl in a History Record Book.

The 1 in. Ordnance Survey Map, Sheet 178, (one copy between two girls) was studied, and the symbols representing different prehistoric earthworks were identified and learnt. These different types of earthwork were described and discussed with the help of coloured slides and of a time-chart to illustrate their place in prehistory. Particular attention was paid to Iron Age hill-forts, their distribution and siting. Written work included listing hill-forts with their grid-references, and planning the route from Sherborne to Dorchester, noting the varied earthworks visible along the way. A detailed study was made of the great fort of Maiden Castle, near Dorchester. We considered its site, construction, history and archaeology, and the life of the people who built it, their homes, agriculture, trade and so on. Then we visited the Dorset County Museum at Dorchester. Each girl was given a plan indicating the show cases relevant to our subject and a quiz to be answered. From there we went to Maiden Castle where the girls were free to roam, ask questions, and take photographs.

My preparation for the work consisted chiefly of liberal use of L. V. Grinsell's *The Archaeology of Wessex* (Methuen, 1958) and a week's participation in the organised excavation of an Iron Age settlement, during which I prepared a small set of slides.

The children enjoyed the archaeological approach. They found the map-work fairly difficult, but the geography mistress worked on it simultaneously, and the effort proved well worthwhile. Several children bought their own maps: five or six cycled regularly during the winter to see hill-forts. Another time I would include the visit to Maiden Castle very early in the work as a stimulus to interest, enquiry and personal observation. Then, to conclude the scheme, we should, if possible, visit a smaller hill-fort to note similarities and variations of site, plan and construction. I should also encourage the children to present their findings in a more vivid and effective way.

(b) Bosham County School, Sussex. Mr. M. E. Colgan and Mrs. P. J. Arnell.

The Bosham Scene in the Bayeux Tapestry: a needlework reproduction, full size and in colour.

The top classes of an all-age school: 45 boys and girls: aged 13-15 years: mixed ability.

This was a special venture in local history which also linked various curriculum subjects.

The work occupied approximately one afternoon and four to six lessons a week for two terms.

The Bosham Scene was copied from the Victoria and Albert Museum's full-size photographs of the Tapestry. The Bayeux Museum helped with information about colours and other details. Relevant publications were obtained from the County Library and elsewhere. The children were fully informed of these preparatory details. Talks and discussions were started, and a plan of work was formed, the children being allocated aspects which they thought they would like to do. Materials were bought—close-woven hessian, coloured wools, etc. The canvas, nine feet long by two feet six inches wide, was placed on stretchers and the outline of the Bosham Scene was copied on to it. The actual needlework was done by six girls at a time working in rotation.

The project snowballed and soon embraced other aspects of local history and other methods of presentation. The boys, working in pairs, made a scale model in balsa of the old part of the village. Booklets were written on topics such as 'The Tapestry Story', 'Bosham Church', 'The Manor of Bosham', and 'Bosham, Now and Then'. These were bound in the handwork class, each page in cellophane. As the work progressed, many items, including old photographs, a copy of the Charter of Bosham, and a Sailing Club burgee, were collected.

A variety of sources was drawn on. The written material consisted of books on the Tapestry, extracts from the *Victoria County History*, articles in *Sussex Archaeological Collections*, histories of the village and church, the R.D.C. Schedule of Buildings of Historic and Architectural Interest, Church Records, the Parish Enclosure Map, and old School Log Books and Admission Registers. The children also obtained information from parents, grandparents, and friends. The Directrice de la Musée de la Tapisserie de la Reine Mathilde at Bayeux showed considerable interest and asked for, and was sent, information by the school.

In the end a halt had to be called as the work could have gone on for years. It aroused considerable interest in the village and information and items useful to the project were often given without being asked for. The children gained by learning more about their locality and forefathers, and still, some years later, recall the experience vividly. I found the work to be the most satisfying teaching experience I have ever had.

(c) Andover Grammar School, Hampshire.

Mr. F. H. Sparrow.

Local History in a G.C.E. O level Course: British History, 1763-1914 (London Board).

Fourth and fifth years: three-form entry, mixed school: 90-100 pupils.

Local history is used chiefly to illustrate and illuminate the course, and is the most valuable of the many aids employed in our teaching. Reference to places well-known to pupils lifts history beyond the text-book level and promotes immeasurably both interest and understanding.

The chief sources used are county, borough and parish records, supplemented by local maps, buildings and places of interest. Most of the basic material was collected by the history master over many years, but sixth-formers and junior school members of the History Club also helped considerably. Many boys and girls have visited the County and Borough

Record Offices, studied old newspapers, traced maps, transcribed documents, and summarised and duplicated records. Original documents are sometimes available in class, by permission of Local Authorities. More frequently, duplicated copies are distributed for individual use. Maps and slides have been prepared. On other occasions, the teacher draws on his own, and the pupils' knowledge of local events. There are many lively, human stories.

With some topics the use of local history is limited to occasional reference. Examples are wars (prisoners of war in the locality), the revolution in textiles (decline of local industry), Radicals (Henry Hunt was an old boy of the school), and tariff reform (a heated local election in 1906). With others, local history is of more direct value. Parliamentary reform, local government, public health, the Corn Laws, periods of distress, the Poor Law, developments in transport, and the whole range of social history—education, religion, housing, sport—all these, and many more, have such a wealth of local material that selection is essential. Two examples will illustrate.

The History Club decided to make a semi-dramatised tape recording about the parliamentary election of 1790 in Hampshire. Members visited record offices and searched newspaper files. The recording begins with a brief reference to the local and national background of the election, continues with a number of local scenes in village, town and manor house, and concludes with a resumé of the campaigns, the exact result, and comments on the whole episode. The script was written by the pupils themselves. The names of the main characters are those who actually participated. The election issues woven into the script were partly national (such as the Test and Corporation Acts and the French Revolution) and partly local (such as the dependence of some freeholders on the squire, the activities of the agents, the scandalous verses written in letters to the local paper, the bribery, and the free food and beer).

The enclosure movement provides a more typical example of our use of local history. Two contrasting local enclosures are studied in detail. In one, the evidence points to land-grabbing at its worst. In the other, reasonable provision seems to have been made for copy- and lease-holders. Source material for the first consists of a pre-enclosure survey, listing tenants and their holdings, and the Enclosure Act and Award. There is no survey for the second, but there is a magnificent pre-enclosure map, a tracing of the award map, and the Award itself. The pre-enclosure map was photographed, and slides are used to show the open field system, the strips and the common land as they actually existed in an adjoining parish. The map also has a special value in that it lists the acreage held by free-, copy- and lease-holders, and the acreage already enclosed by agreement fifty years before the Enclosure Act. The enclosure map has been traced from the Quarter Sessions Journal and the tracing photographed. In spite of different scales, it is easy for pupils to see exactly what enclosure really was. Teaching normally proceeds from these two villages to others in the area, then to the rest of the county, then to the national scene. So much interest has been aroused that many children have studied their own parish awards and stimulated a lively response from parents and friends.

The time spent on local history certainly has no adverse effect on our examination results: indeed, it gives a new interest and meaning to much of the work which are reflected in the pupils' essays.

(d) Western Secondary School, Southampton.

Miss K. B. Chapple.

Work on Original Documents in the Southampton Civic Record Office.

A small G.C.E. group of six to ten boys and girls, aged 16, does this work during its final year in this non-grammar secondary school.

The aims of the work are (i) to enable the children to handle and study original documents which are easy to read, and (ii) to provide specific local evidence to illustrate general themes in their G.C.E. syllabus.

One visit is made, lasting 2½ hours. 1½ hours are spent working on the records: the rest of the time is taken up watching the record-repairer at work and examining some of the city's most valuable records.

Detailed arrangements for the visit are made beforehand with the City Archivist. Its nature and purpose are also explained to the children in advance. One or two documents are allotted to each child, according to interest and ability, together with a list of questions to be answered from them. Page references are given. The G.C.E. syllabus followed combines a topic (History of the Commonwealth) with a period (The Victorian Age). Documents relevant to these themes which have been used include a map and inventory of a Nevis sugar plantation; material relating to emigration to Melbourne; Guardians of the Poor minute books; Board of Health minute books and report on cholera; and a Southampton-Dorset Railway prospectus.

Questions set on the map of Nevis were as follows: (1) What is the date of the survey? (2) Who is the owner of the plantation? (3) Describe the different parts of the plantation. (4) Name two crops grown. (5) What is the meaning of 'Small-pox piece'? Those relating to the inventory of the plantation were: (1) What is the name of the owner? (2) What is the date of the inventory? (3) What is a 'still'? (4) What is the plantation's value, excluding negroes? (5) What is the price of (a) the most valuable, (b) the least valuable, negro? (6) Find out what 'rattoon canes' were. (7) Make a list of animals mentioned.

I check their answers and give help, if necessary, as they work, but I do not keep a formal record for myself. I hope that they will use the local information gained to illustrate general answers.

I believe the work to be extremely valuable with more able children; the less able tire more quickly, although they often change documents, if necessary. The more able complain that they hardly have time to get started: another difficulty lies in finding documents of comparable interest and value. I have found that the map and inventory stimulate most interest and would think that more work of a topographical nature might prove rewarding in future. This approach could be easily adapted for work in school, instead of in a record office, by the use of photo-copies of local documents.

(e) Portsmouth Grammar School. Mr. A. J. Marsh.

Aspects of Naval History.

Sixth form: 2 or 3 boys.

Portsmouth owes its growth so much to the navy that any concentration on local studies leads ultimately to the navy and its needs. A valuable exercise is undertaken each year by a few senior boys who have the opportunity, through the kind co-operation of the Trustees and officers, of studying in the Manuscript Room of the National Maritime Museum at Greenwich.

After the A level examination in the summer term, three days are spent at Greenwich, and a varying amount of time is subsequently devoted to the work.

The boys who go are either historians or boys intending to join the navy. About a fortnight before their visit, the school sends a list of topics which the boys would prefer to study, but they are strongly encouraged to accept the guidance of the Custodian of the Manuscripts. He may report that he has little of value on a chosen topic and suggest another which seems promising. It is wise, as well as courteous, to accept this advice. The boy who insists that he wants to study, say, 'The Evidence of Corruption in the Elizabethan Navy' gets what he deserves—practically nothing.

The time at the Museum is spent examining and transcribing documents. The school gives a small allowance for buying copies of prints, charts, documents or ship-plans, and the boys usually supplement this from their own pockets. They then return to school and during the remainder of the term, and in the holidays, produce finished articles, after doing further reading of printed material to put their own research into some perspective. Though the boys have often left school before this work is complete, they have, in nearly every case, produced their articles imaginatively laid out, illustrated and bound, and running to forty to sixty pages. The school then sends the finished articles to Greenwich, and the Custodian of Manuscripts has been generous of his time in reading them and returning them to the boys with his comments and criticisms.

Subjects chosen have all been from the seventeenth and eighteenth centuries. Earlier material tends to be fragmentary and hard to decipher; later material may be too voluminous to be dealt with in three days. Boys have produced work on the following: Battles of the Second Dutch War; The Rochefort Raid, 1757; the Career of Captain Clements; A Survey of the Activities of Portsmouth Dockyard, 1754-7; The Voyages of Captain Philip Carteret; and The Landing on Belleisle, 1761.

Eighteenth century naval documents offer a relatively easy and exciting introduction to the study of original material. The events are dramatic in themselves, the professional jargon and abbreviations are soon mastered, and the sea-dogs express themselves with forthright vigour in a bold hand. In three days a student can trace a small naval operation through a variety of documents—Admiral's Order Book, ships' log books, Dockyard Commissioner's Letters and, possibly, private journals and letters.

The number of suitable topics is limited, and this type of research, which demands much of the Museum staff, can obviously only be offered to a few people at a time. For larger parties, the National Maritime Museum is prepared to arrange short lectures backed by special displays of pictures, models and documents on particular subjects.

(f) St. Andrew's C. of E. Secondary School for Boys, Worthing, Sussex.

Mr. R. W. H. Dolman, Mr. J. Brooke and Mr. T. W. Hearl.

Clifton Road Survey, 1790-1959.

Fifth year secondary modern: 18 boys: aged 16 years: rather above average ability.

The objects of this survey were both educational and historical Educationally, the survey gave boys who had studied between three and six subjects to G.C.E. O level, an opportunity to put their knowledge and training to a practical test. Historically, it added to known information about the neighbourhood and produced a permanent pictorial and written record of local features which were about to be swept away.

The three weeks after the summer O level examination were spent on this work.

A row of sixteen early nineteenth century workers' cottages opposite the school was awaiting demolition. The 5th year pupils were asked to produce a historical survey of the street's development, an accurate plan and elevation of one typical cottage, a pictorial record in water-colour and pencil sketches of the buildings, a photographic record of the site and demolition, a natural history survey of the gardens, and a survey of the road's use today. This work was to be presented in two forms: firstly, as a School Exhibition, the material to be later made available to Worthing Library's 'Sussex Collection'; and secondly, as a 22-page illustrated foolscap booklet, of which eighty duplicated and bound copies were produced by the pupils. Typing excepted, all this work was performed by the boys with the minimum direction from the staff.

The historical background material was drawn from manorial, enclosure and other local maps; directories, guidebooks and newspapers; and documentary sources which included deeds, sale catalogues, parish registers, church rate returns, borough records, census returns, parliamentary pollbooks, and voters' registers. The guidance of the librarian of the local reference library was essential. Interviewing old inhabitants brought further interesting details to light. Much of this information has since been used in the school's history lessons.

This survey was followed by Broadwater Cottage Survey (1960); Highdown: a Field Survey (1961); and Railway Approach Development Survey (assisting a Worthing Museum

Study, 1963). The method of operation was the same in each case. The 5th year class was encouraged to use its initiative within the broad terms of reference set. The main stipulations were that a complete written report must be produced, all work must be accurate, and, wherever possible, new knowledge must be gained. Pupils undertaking the Highdown survey chose to use colour-film and tape-recorder. The result was a set of colour transparencies accompanied by a recorded commentary and interviews with a local geologist, naturalist, landowner and farmers.

Although the advent of external examinations provided the first opportunity for these surveys, it is becoming increasingly difficult to undertake work of this nature owing to the enormous increase in both the number of examinations and the number of boys involved.

(g) Hamble County Secondary School, Hampshire.

Mr. P. D. Dutton.

Hamble Village: Some Changes in the Last Hundred Years.

Third year retarded class: thirteen boys and seven girls: average age 14 years, 4 months: I.Q. 58-73.

The work formed part of an otherwise fairly formal chronological course based on R. J. Unstead, *Looking at History: Queen Anne to Queen Elizabeth II* (Black).

Six weeks. One morning a week was spent in the village, plus an additional visit in each of the last two weeks. The village lies just over a mile from the school: some pupils cycled, others went by bus. During the first three weeks, four lessons (two hours) a week were spent on the work in class; during the last three weeks, anything up to eight lessons a week. The time varied with the pupil.

The work that we did on Hamble was probably our most successful effort that year. It arose out of lessons on social conditions in Victorian England. We turned to work on the neighbourhood because I wanted the class to know something about local conditions a hundred years ago and because I wanted to vary my methods by getting the boys and girls working outside the classroom. I copied the extract describing the village from W. White, *History, Gazetteer and Directory of the County of Hampshire* (2nd ed., 1878) and also listed the names, addresses, and occupations of all the people mentioned. Each child had a copy of this information. We all went down to the churchyard for the first lesson, a whole morning, to see if we could find any of the names on our list recorded on the gravestones. We searched the burial ground fairly systematically, drew interesting stones, and copied their inscriptions. We found several of the names we were looking for: we were also diverted on to other lines of enquiry. The grave of Sir Alliott Verdon Roe gave rise to lessons on early aviation. A stone commemorating the death of five children within a few months of one another led us to discuss public health, sanitation and diseases. One boy found the name of a relative and, with his grandmother's help, managed to construct a family tree. Then we looked for, and found, some of the houses in which the people had lived. Many drawings were made. The names of the streets and roads were listed and their derivations traced, where possible. We also drew a large-scale map and painted in the houses and the street names. The *Directory* entry on Hamble School resulted in lessons on schools and schooling past and present. Finally, the pupils were encouraged to talk to householders, to ask about their houses, and to find out what Hamble used to be like. We were very lucky in that one house, now a café, was full of interest, and that the proprietor was a very friendly and understanding person. We always met there for drinks or ices when we had finished our work and made it a social occasion.

I had been taking this class for nearly two years. We knew one another well and, when they were out of school, they did not misbehave and worked hard. They enjoyed themselves and felt that they were doing something useful, adult and real. Teaching them, and being with them on the visits, was a pleasure. I am sure that we all gained a lot from the work, not least in social behaviour in and around the village. One boy remarked to a group, 'I didn't know Hamble could be so interesting'. For the first time many realised what makes up their environment. It was very satisfying.

The only real problem that I encountered was in deciding the accuracy of some of the information collected. Next time I shall spend longer on such work and include more interviews with people like the Vicar and elderly residents. We shall also pay more attention to present problems and try to produce a simple directory of the modern village.

(h) The John Pounds Portsea Secondary Modern School for Girls, Portsmouth. Miss B. M. Bray.

The Story of Portsmouth: A Study of a Living Community.

The whole school: 350 girls, aged 11-16.

One morning a week for a term (14 weeks) was spent on this work which took the place of Geography and History with some forms and of English and History with others.

The following notes were issued to all teachers:

'The aim of the course is to study Portsmouth as a living community, to discover how this community of a quarter of a million people has come into being and to examine some of the many aspects of its varied life. The emphasis throughout should be on those aspects of local history which help to throw light on the present character of the city. It is also important that students should be encouraged to play as big a part as possible. A good deal of the information is not available in text books and can be obtained only by research, by visits to places of interest, and from speakers visiting the school. All of this offers opportunity for varied methods of teaching and for the development of study techniques on the part of the students. These opportunities need to be fully exploited, and the success of the course needs to be measured in terms of active student participation.

'Throughout, teachers can bear in mind the possibility of an exhibition on the whole project. The keeping of note-books, the recording of interviews, and the illustration of places by drawings and photographs offer considerable scope. However, the important thing is not the exhibition which may ultimately result so much as the incentive which it offers to active participation. It may be possible to have a conference in which scholars and teachers report to the whole school on the work they have undertaken and the exhibition material they have been able to collect.

'This work presents many opportunities for visits to places of interest, and for visiting speakers with specialised knowledge to come to school. Care should be taken to obtain the maximum benefit from these: they should not be regarded as an interruption of the normal classroom work. Students should be prepared for what they are going to hear, they should be helped to formulate questions beforehand, and they should be encouraged to produce a record of what transpires. It is also of great help when inviting a visiting speaker to discuss the subject with the class in advance and to formulate some questions which should be sent to the speaker. The more guidance that can be given to the speaker the better. It is also necessary for the girls to be prepared for what they are to look for when they go out on visits.

'Again, the course will be valuable in so far as we can encourage curiosity on the part of the student. After all, we are to study a community of which she is a part and in which some aspects of its life are within her experience. It is important to stimulate enquiry, to make students ask questions and, above all, to encourage them to use their eyes.'

Each form chose a topic and worked under the direction of the form teacher. The teachers received prior help from an historian who supplied bibliographies and lists of suggested visits. Co-operation from officials such as the Town Clerk, City Librarian, and Archivist, enabled us to have access to ancient buildings, Council meetings, historic documents, etc. The topics studied were: Education, Industries, Transport, Law and Order, The Care of the Sick, Entertainments, The Harbour, The Sea Shore, The Dockyard, The Early Story of Portsea, The

Story of Southsea, Churches, Monuments, Famous Places, and Famous People.

The work on 'Industries' illustrates the methods used. Pairs of girls from the third year B stream visited most of the large firms in the city. They wrote for permission (unknown to them, I enclosed a covering letter explaining the purpose and value of the project), and then went to seek the answers to a series of questions worked out in class. They wrote letters of thanks and compiled folders of their findings. They toured the Harbour, saw film-strips, and listened to visiting speakers. They were out of school a good deal: they also did a lot of work in their own time.

An exhibition on 'The Living Community' was shown to parents, and the girls told visitors what they had learned. They also explained it to every form in the school, so that everyone knew a little of what the others had done.

The project was, I think, successful in that the more academic girls carried out lengthy investigations while the less able enjoyed it, too, and were able to work within their capability. It produced an attitude of enquiry; it necessitated the purposeful use of books; it gave each girl a turn at explaining her form's work. The school is in a very under-privileged part of Portsmouth where natural interest in one's surroundings is foreign to those who live there: I felt that this work stirred up an interest in, and loyalty to, the City which most of the girls taking part had not experienced before. It also helped to build a much-needed bridge between the work of the school and the local community. Employers and industrialists were very co-operative and interested in what the girls were doing: most of them not only gave the girls the information they asked for, but also lent material and came to the exhibition. Grandparents and great-grandparents also recalled old places and events for us. These memories were exciting to listen to and share. When we undertook a similar survey four years ago the interest in such recollections was so keen that we decided to become John Pounds School: up to then we were merely Portsea Modern. This grafting of tradition has done a great deal for our school, and it grew naturally from the girls' interest in his work for their ancestors.

Local History Studies in School and College

(i) Poole Grammar School, Dorset. Mr. N. H. Field.

A School Archaeological Society.

This school's Archaeological Society was founded in 1951 and has been active ever since. According to the type of activity, boys of all ages from 11 or 12 to 18 or 19 have taken part. At indoor meetings, numbers are usually between twenty-five and thirty, but outdoors, they must usually be limited to a dozen at the maximum unless we are simply visiting a site. The Society has always been an out-of-school activity, since the writer teaches modern languages. However, it inaugurated and stocked the School Museum case for the History Room with specimens from its field work and, for one boy with an exceptional interest in archaeology from the age of 11, the A level special subject, 'Roman Britain', was arranged by his history master.

What should be the aims and scope of a school archaeological society? The writer has found that such a society must divide its outdoor activities into two groups, (i) excavation, with all that it entails; and (ii) visiting, recording and measuring new, and old, sites and monuments without excavation. As an example of the former, the excavation of the Romano-British settlement at Studland was carried on for seven consecutive seasons. This excavation is described in a report which appeared in the *Proceedings of the Dorset Natural History and Archaeological Society*, vol. lxxxvii (1965). Experience shows that, though the advice of experts can always be readily obtained, responsibility for final publication (and excavation without publication is a 'crime') must be the teacher's. This means that most of the recording, drawing, and production of the typescript must again be his, though older boys will often be very helpful at different stages, once they have had some experience. Younger boys can be shown how to trowel, how to recognise significant layers, what must be put on the tray, what must be left where it is. Help can be given later in sorting finds and in arranging displays that may be required at archaeological meetings. Clearly then, no teacher should undertake excavation without both training and the sustained conviction that he is going to give much of his private time to archaeology. Group (ii) activities are less exacting in their demands on the teacher. In this category, the Society has, in recent years, recorded discoveries made by modern trenching machines and kept a watchful eye on threats to monuments from development.

Indoor activities sometimes arise from excavation: they have included piecing pottery from digs; preparing exhibits for the School Museum; and exhibiting finds and projecting slides at Wessex regional conferences of the Council for British Archaeology. Other meetings have been devoted to 'Animal, Vegetable, Mineral' sessions with material to identify from Poole Museum, archaeological films, and lectures.

The writer likes to think that the several hundred boys who have, at one time or another, dug with the School Archaeological Society have enjoyed their acquaintance with the disinterested pursuit of this branch of learning: certainly two (at Cardiff and Oxford Universities) are on the way to making archaeology a career. Interest aroused by the Society also often leads to discoveries on the ground since boys use their eyes when passing pipe trenches or ploughed land.

Some Useful Lists

(i) MORE SUGGESTIONS FOR LOCAL WORK

The examples given on pp. 137-197 contain many ideas which can be used in a variety of ways and at different educational levels. The following assorted catalogue briefly mentions some others of which the writer has personal experience. Many of the books listed on pp. 200-202 also include examples of work which has been undertaken.

Measured plans: classroom, playground, farmyard, houses, church, etc.

Cross-sections and sketches: of landscape and individual features.

Scale-models of neighbourhood: in papier-maché, plaster or using 25 in. O.S. plan as a base.

Route studies: identifying and answering questions about specific items (*cf.* nature trails).

Large time charts: with columns for national, regional and local events.

Friezes, composite pictures and dioramas.

General work on specific periods, using local sources: for example, 'Our Village in the Middle Ages', 'A Royal Progress of Elizabeth I', 'The Civil War in Hampshire'. The last two hundred years offer plentiful relevant material and are often neglected: 'Life when Father/Grandfather was a Boy' or changes in any of the social services or means of communication are rewarding topics.

More restricted attempts at similar work: for example, tracing boundaries of land-grants on a modern map and on the ground; making charters with cartridge paper soaked in milk and gently heated in the oven; meanings of local place names and surnames of children in class; writing stories, plays, eye-witness accounts and newspaper descriptions of events from local records. For suggestions for work arising from specific classes of record, such as Domesday Book, manorial records, parish records, etc., see J. West, *Village Records* (Macmillan, 1962), pp. 187-193.

Study of selected records for their interest as documents: language, handwriting, seals.

Buildings' studies: as basis for history studies in a building or technical school; housing patterns; architectural details; demolition of buildings as lessons in appreciation or idea of change; Junior Civic Trust survey of signs; planning; an individual building, especially an old church, as a time-line; a building or ruin as an example of a type; the church as a study in social history; the school; industrial archaeology.

Brass rubbings: for own interest or for study of costume and armour.

Studies of heraldic emblems.

Collections of 'old' local historical items: general or confined, for example, to books, coins, costume, documents, fossils, medals, newspapers, ornaments, pictures, tools, utensils, etc.

Talks by local experts: archivists, curators, local government officials, etc.; small exhibitions of material brought by them; extension of Schools Loan Service.

Compilation of scrapbooks recording aspects of the contemporary local scene and chronology of events.

Photographic surveys, slides, films and film-strips.

Tape recordings of old and young: stories and dialect; customs, games, rhymes, field-names, etc.

Local personalities: their importance and local connections.

Local places which visitors come to see: why?

Exchange studies with a school in another area: if possible, exchange visits.

Local work in subjects other than history, for example biology, geography and rural studies would often be improved if more consideration were given to historical aspects. Similarly, more investigations which take the environment, and not a subject, as the starting point need to be undertaken.

(ii) A SELECT LIST OF BOOKS, ARTICLES AND ADDRESSES RELATING TO LOCAL HISTORY STUDIES IN SCHOOL AND COLLEGE

Many of these sources contain examples of local work which has been undertaken at various educational levels.

J. R. Armstrong and P. G. H. Hopkins, *Local Studies* (Workers' Educational Association and Workers' Educational Trade Union Committee, 1955).

Association of Assistant Mistresses, *Curriculum, Eleven to Eighteen* (University of London Press, 1949).

H. E. Bracey, *Village Survey* and *Country Town Survey* (Methuen, 1953 and 1954).

C. V. Butler, *Village Survey Making: an Oxfordshire Experiment* (H.M.S.O., 1929).

J. K. Dale, *Introducing Local Studies* (Dent, 1956).

R. G. Dawes *et al.*, 'Local Studies in Practice', *Educational Review*, no. vi (1953).

M. S. Dilke ed., *Field Studies for Schools: The Purpose and Organisation of Field Studies* (Rivingtons, 1965).

I. Doncaster, *Finding the History Around Us* (Oxford, Blackwell, 1956).

I. Doncaster, *Discovering Man's Habitat* (National Froebel Foundation, 1963).

R. Douch, 'Local History in School: An Experiment by the University of Southampton Institute of Education', *The Amateur Historian*, vol. vi., no. 7 (1965).

R. Douch, 'Time to Take Stock? Training College Studies and Local History', *Education for Teaching*, no. 53 (1960).

R. Douch and F. W. Steer, *Local History Essays: Some Notes for Students* (University of Southampton Institute of Education, 1960).

F. Evans *et al.*, *Local Studies for Schools* (4th ed., Philip, 1962).

F. H. Fraser, 'Local and Environmental Studies for ESN Children', *Special Education*, vol. liii, no. 2 (Summer, 1964).

Geographical Association, *Local Studies: Schemes of Work . . .* (2nd ed., Geographical Association, 1949).

R. C. Hayward, 'The Study of Local History', *History*, vol. xxxi (1946).

Hull University College, Institute of Education, 'School and Neighbourhood', *Studies in Education*, vol. i, no. 5 (1951).

D. W. Humphreys and F. G. Emmison, *Local History for Students* (National Council of Social Service, 1966).

E. Layton and J. B. White, *The School Looks Around: A Book for Teachers about Local Surveys* (Longmans, 1948).

R. F. Mackenzie, *A Question of Living* (Collins, 1963).

T. H. McGuffie, 'History and Local Studies', *The Schoolmaster*, 13th June-18th July, 1958.

T. H. McGuffie, *The World and You: Teachers' Reference Book* (Chatto and Windus, 1950).

H. McNicol, *History, Heritage and Environment* (Faber, 1946).

F. E. Melton, *Local Lore* (Nelson, History Practice Supplement, no. i, n.d.).

Ministry of Education, *Local Studies* (H.M.S.O., 1948).

N. Moorsom, 'Local History in a Town School', *The Amateur Historian*, vol. vi, no. 7 (1965).

P. Northeast, 'Local History in a Village School', *The Amateur Historian*, vol. vi, no. 7 (1965).

W. H. Shercliff, 'The Use of Local History Materials in Education', *Library World*, June, 1963.

J. E. Short and J. H. Cook, 'An Experiment in the Application of an Environmental Study to the Teaching of History', *History*, vol. xxxviii (1953).

T. H. Simms, 'A Plea for Historical Research in the Training College', *History*, vol. xxxii (1947).

V. H. T. Skipp, 'Amateur Study of Local History', *The Amateur Historian*, vol. vi, no. 6 (1965).

E. Stones, 'Local Sources in the Study and Teaching of Industrial History', *Vocational Aspect of Secondary and Further Education*, vol. ix (1957).

A. E. Tubbs, 'Local Surveys: Purpose and Planning' and 'Local Studies', *Educational Review*, vol. i, no. i (1948) and vol. iv, no. 2 (1952).

E. C. Walker, *History Teaching for Today* (Nisbet, 1935).

J. Walton, 'Historical Field Studies in Secondary Education', *Forum*, vol. ii (1959).

J. West, 'The History of Here', *The Teacher*, 4th Sept.-16th October, 1964.

S. H. Zoeftig, 'These Juniors Go Exploring in History', *Forum,* vol. ii (1960).

School Library Association, *Using Books in the Primary School* (The Association, 1962).

W. H. Shercliff, 'The School and the Local History Library', *Manchester Review,* Summer, 1960.

L. V. Grinsell, 'Children and Archaeology', *Museums Journal,* vol. lx (1960).

F. G. Emmison, *Archives and Local History* (Methuen, 1966).

E. R. Lloyd, 'The Use of Historical Documents in Schools', *The Amateur Historian,* vol. vii, no. 2 (1966).

E. H. Sargeant *et al.*, 'County Archives and Education', *Educational Review,* vol. v, no. 1 (1952).

W. E. Tate, 'The Use of Archives in Education', *Archives,* vol. i (1949).

M. Harrison, *Learning Out of School: A Brief Guide to the Educational Use of Museums* (Educational Supply Association, 1954).

B. Winstanley, *School-Loan Services* (Museums Association, 1959).

E. M. Jones, 'Film Strips for Local History', *Times Educational Supplement,* 19th October, 1956.

H. A. Taylor, 'Local History: an Experiment with Slides and Tapes', *Archives,* vol. v (1962).

See also W. H. Burston and C. W. Green eds., *Handbook for History Teachers* (Methuen, 1962) and the University of Southampton Institute of Education booklist, *The Teaching of Geography, History and Related Local Studies* (2nd ed., The Institute, 1957).

ADDRESSES

Many of the associations and organisations, the addresses of which have been given in Part II, are actively concerned with educational work. Among these may be mentioned local institutions such as libraries, record offices and museums which often have special facilities and publications for children, and national bodies like the Geographical Association, the Historical Association and the Field Studies Council. The Ministry of Public Building and Works issues free permits for educational visits to monuments and buildings in its care.

The following addresses may also be of interest:

THE ASSOCIATION FOR EDUCATION IN CITIZENSHIP, 14, KENDALL PLACE, LONDON, W.1. publishes book-lists and pamphlets.

THE EDUCATIONAL FOUNDATION FOR VISUAL AIDS IN EDUCATION, 33, Queen Anne Street, London, W.1. publishes catalogues of films and filmstrips.

THE GROUP FOR CHILDREN'S ACTIVITIES IN MUSEUMS, THE CITY MUSEUM, QUEEN'S ROAD, BRISTOL, 8. promotes various activities and publishes a *Register of Schools Service Facilities in the British Isles.*

THE NATIONAL RURAL STUDIES ASSOCIATION, 29, WOODHALL CLOSE, BENGEO, HERTFORD, HERTS.

(iii) LOCAL HISTORY STUDIES: BOOKS FOR CHILDREN

The books listed, like most of those published in these categories, are designed for older junior and/or secondary school pupils. Further details can be obtained from local librarians or publishers' catalogues.

(*a*) *Some General Works*

K. V. Bailey, *Exploring the Past* (Studio Vista).

E. Blishen and J. C. Armitage, *Town Story*, 3 vols. (Blond Educational).

G. J. Copley, *Going into the Past* (Phoenix House).

J. X. W. P. Corcoran, *The Young Field Archaeologist's Guide* (Bell).

H. J. Deverson and R. Lampitt, *The Map that Came to Life* (Oxford University Press).

G. S. Fletcher, *Town's Eye View* (Hutchinson).

G. Grigson, *Looking and Finding* (Phoenix House).

K. A. Lindley, *Town, Time and People* (Phoenix House).
E. W. Martin, *The Book of the Village* (Phoenix House).
E. W. Martin, *The Book of the Country Town* (Phoenix House).
E. Osmond, *A Valley Grows Up* (Oxford University Press).
P. J. Randall, *Treasure on Your Doorstep* (Pitman).
F. W. Robins, *On the Track of the Past* (Phoenix House).
P. A. Sauvain, *Exploring at Home* (Hulton).
W. A. Smallcombe, *Archaeology for Young People* (Harrap).
W. E. Tate, *His Worship the Mayor* (Oxford University Press).
W. E. Tate and C. Blount, *British Institutions* (Oxford University Press).
C. Trent, *Exploring the Countryside* (Phoenix House).
J. N. T. Vince, *History All Around You* (Wheaton).
W. P. Westell and K. Harvey, *Look and Find Out: Unwritten History and How to Read It* (Macmillan).

Council for British Archaeology, *British Archaeology: a Book-list* (The Council, 1960): Part II deals with children's books.

(*b*) *Some Series of Reference Books*

Picture Source Books for Social History, Understanding the Modern World (Allen and Unwin).
St. George's Library (Ed. Arnold).
Rockliff New Project Histories (Barrie and Rockliff).
Everyday Life, Everyday Things, Junior Heritage, Styles of English Architecture (Batsford).
Reference Books (Black).
Know About (Blackie).
Learning Library, How They Lived, Pocket Histories, They Saw It Happen, Who's Who in History (Blackwell and Mott).
Men of the Counties, Study Books (Bodley Head).
Picture Reference Books (Brockhampton Press).
How Long Have They Helped Us, Journeys Through Our Early History, Things We Need (Bruce and Gawthorn).
Jackdaws (Cape).
Dawn of History, Look at the Past, Man's Forward March, Open Your Eyes Picture Books (Chatto and Windus).

I-Spy (Dickens).
Young Farmers' Club Booklets (Evans).
The Story of . . ., Your Book of . . . (Faber).
History Bookshelves, Museum Bookshelves (Ginn).
Look Books (Hamish Hamilton).
The Story of . . . , Britain Told in Pictures (Hope and Sankey Hudson).
Children in History (Hulton).
As We Were, Evidence in Pictures, Man's Heritage, Live and Learn, Then and There (Longmans).
Rathbone Books Wonderful World (Macdonald).
Get to Know, Outlines (Methuen).
Exploring the Past, Junior True Books, Let's Look at . . ., True Books (Muller).
The Changing Shape of Things (Murray).
Instructions to . . . (Museum Press).
Open Gate Library, Signpost Library (Oliver and Boyd).
History Through the Ages, How They Were Built, Oxford Junior Encyclopaedia, People of the Past (Oxford University Press).
Puffin Picture Books (Penguin Books).
Excursion (Phoenix House).
How (Routledge and Kegan Paul).
Discovery Reference Books (University of London Press).
How Things Are Made, How Things Developed, How to Explore, People's Jobs (Ward Lock Educational).
Observer's Books (Warne).
Read About It (Wheaton).

(iv) SOME EXAMPLES OF AIDS TO THE STUDY OF PARTICULAR LOCALITIES

The teacher's task would often be easier if more aids to the study of his particular locality were available. Various aids have been produced recently in different parts of the country, some examples of which are listed below. A variety of organisations and individuals, such as local societies, local authority departments, Institutes of Education and teachers' groups, has been responsible for the compilation and publication of this material. There is boundless scope for enlarging these activities and, in particular, for teachers to combine with librarians, curators and archivists in the production of such aids.

(*a*) *General Guides to Sources*

T. Booth and H. A. Carnell eds., *Local History in Bedfordshire. A Handbook of Guidance upon Sources and Materials available for Teachers and Historians* (Bedfordshire Co. Co., 1960).

R. Douch, *A Handbook of Local History: Dorset, with a Suplement of Additions and Corrections to 1960* (University of Bristol, 1962).

C. D. B. Ellis, *History in Leicester, 55 B.C.-A.D. 1900* (Leicester Information Department, Backus, 1948).

M. B. Honeybourne, *The History of London: Notes on a Course for Secondary Modern Schools* (Historical Association, n.d.).

N. J. Frangopulo ed., *Rich Inheritance: A Guide to the History of Manchester* (Manchester Education Committee, 1963).

H. A. Taylor comp., *Northumberland History* (Northumberland Co. Co., 1963).

See also the published *Catalogues* to the Local History Collections of public libraries.

Many museums have Schools' Officers whose job it is to develop the educational side of their institutions' work. One or two record offices, such as Essex and Kent, have similar appointments.

(*b*) *Guides to Specific Types of Sources*

In addition to the bibliographies, surveys and series describing particular types of sources which have been listed in Part II, the following may be mentioned.

Several collections of descriptions of geographical field excursions for schools have been published concerning, for example, the London area (London University Institute of Education); Surrey (K. S. Wheeler and M. Harding eds.,

Geographical Fieldwork. A Handbook, Blond Educational, 1965); the north-east Midlands (Nottingham University Institute of Education); north-west England (Rivingtons, for the Manchester University School of Education); and Yorkshire (Leeds University Institute of Education). These usually contain some information and ideas for history teachers. See also *History Field Studies in the Durham Area* (Durham University Institute of Education, 1966).

J. W. L. Forge ed., *List of Antiquities in the Administrative County of Surrey* (Surrey Co. Co., 1965).

A. C. Edwards, *English History from Essex Sources, 1550-1750* and A. F. J. Brown, *English History from Essex Sources, 1750-1900* (Chelmsford, Clarke, 1952) are valuable collections of local documents illustrating and explaining national movements and events.

(c) *Series of Booklets*

Useful series include those published by:

Local Authorities: *e.g. Chichester Papers, Southampton Papers.*

Local Libraries, Museums and Record Offices: details can be obtained from G. A. Williams comp., *Guide to Sources of Illustrative Material for Use in Teaching History* (Historical Association, 1962) and from individual institutions: see, for example, the publications of the Manchester and Sheffield City Libraries, the Chester and Lincoln Museums, and the Essex and Kent County Record Offices. Photostat copies of documents, maps, cards, broadsheets and slides may also be available.

Local History Societies: *e.g.* Eccles and District History Society, East Yorkshire Local History Society.

Branches of the Historical Association: *e.g.* Bristol, Coventry.

Extra-Mural Classes: *e.g.* V. H. T. Skipp, *Discovering Sheldon* (University of Birmingham, Department of Extra-Mural Studies, 1960); Upminster Local History Group, *The Story of Upminster,* 14 booklets and *Index* (Upminster, The Group, 1957-64); L. M. Munby, *History of King's Langley* (Workers' Educational Association, 1963).

(*d*) *Archive Teaching Units*

These Units were first seriously developed by the University of Sheffield Institute of Education in co-operation with the Sheffield City Library. Such units consist of photocopies of documents and maps, supported by background notes and work sheets, for class use in primary and secondary schools. Local topics of national significance, such as 'The Yorkshire Election of 1807' and 'The Sheffield-Wakefield Turnpike Road', were covered. Localities for which archive teaching units have been subsequently produced include Liverpool (Liverpool Teachers Archive Study Group), Nottingham (University Department of Manuscripts) and Worcestershire (City of Worcester College of Education).

(*e*) *Books Written for Children*

The following list illustrates a variety of interesting approaches.

W. A. Richardson, *Our Birmingham* (2nd ed., University of London Press, 1950).

J. and B. Blake, *The Story of Carlisle* (Carlisle Education Committee, 1958).

W. A. Richardson, *Citizen's Derby* (University of London Press, 1949).

W. G. Hoskins, *Devon and its People* (Wheaton, 1959).

R. R. Sellman, *Illustrations of Devon History* (Methuen, 1962).

R. R. Sellman, *Illustrations of Dorset History* (Methuen, 1960).

P. Thornhill, *Downs and Weald* (3rd ed., Christophers, 1950).

L. J. Redstone, *Our East Anglian Heritage* (2nd ed., Methuen, 1951).

W. G. S. Crook, *A Child's Hertfordshire Reader* (E. J. Arnold, 1956).

H. W. Saunders, *Aids and Suggestions for the Teaching of Local History with special reference to Rural Schools in Kent* (Maidstone, Kent Co. Co., 1922).

E. I. Abell and J. D. Chambers, *The Story of Lincoln* (Lincoln Education Committee, 1939).

Manchester Branch, Historical Association, *Portfolio of Illus-*

trations relating to the History of Manchester and Salford and the Surrounding District (1932).

P. W. Blake *et al., The Norfolk We Live In* (Norwich, Jarrold, 1958).

P. J. Harris and P. W. Hartop, *Northamptonshire: its Land and People* (40 King Edward Road, Northampton, 1950).

H. J. Sparks, *The Story of Portsmouth* (Portsmouth Education Committee, 1921).

M. Hinton, *A History of the Town of Reading* (Harrap, 1954).

L. A. Burgess and H. S. Faircloth, *Historical Perspectives of Southampton* (Southampton Education Committee, 1954).

H. Bowling, L. C. Coombes and R. Walker, *The Land of the Three Rivers: the Tyne, the Wear and the Tees* (Macmillan, 1958).

E. M. Fletcher, *Our Yorkshire* (Ripon, Wakeman Press, 1951).

E. M. Fletcher, *Youngsters in Yorkshire: Local History for the Family*, 3 vols. (Hull, Brown, 1948-57).

See also Council for British Archaeology, *British Archaeology. A Booklist* (The Council, 1960), pp. 41-43 and such series as *Illustrated County Histories* (Darwen Finlayson).

(f) *Some Published Histories Written by Students in Schools and Colleges*

Aspley Heath School, Historical Society, *A History of Our District (Aspley Guise, Aspley Heath, Battlesden . . .). Revised and enlarged by the scholars of Fulbrook Secondary School* (Aspley Guise, The Powage Press, 1962).

J. W. Crick *et al., Two Parishes—One Village, by the Village Schoolmaster and his Senior Scholars . . . Offord Cluny and Offord Darcy, Huntingdonshire* (Huntingdon, Gogg, 1951).

W. C. Farr ed., *Merchant Taylors' School: its Origin, History and Present Surroundings* (Oxford, Blackwell, 1929).

F. W. Headley and W. Kennedy, *The Country round Haileybury* (Cambridge University Press, privately printed, 1920).

Hele's Grammar School, Historical Society, *Exeter Then and Now* (Exeter, Wheaton).

Hockerill Training College, *Bishop's Stortford* (Rev. ed., Le Play House Press, 1948).

Knutton County Secondary Modern School, Newcastle-under-Lyme, *Newcastle—Yesterday, Today, Tomorrow* (Newcastle, 1958).

The Leys School, Cambridge, *Horningsea, 1949-50. A Survey of a Cambridgeshire Village* (The School, 1952).

Wakefield Cathedral Secondary School, *Quick Quiz Local Surveys: Wakefield* (The School, 1963).

R. J. Whiteman ed., *Hexton: a Parish Survey, made and compiled by the Senior Scholars of Herts. Co. Co. School, Hexton* (Privately printed, 1936).

Willerby, Carr Lane School, *A Survey of Willerby and Kirk Ella; prepared by the Senior Scholars* (The School, 1951).

Winchester College Archaeological Society, *Winchester College: its History, Buildings and Customs* (Winchester, Wells, 1926).

York, Bootham School Natural History and Archaeological Societies, *Two Country Parishes . . . Skelton and Averton* (The School, 1956).

Index

Authors, book titles, most societies and 'Examples of Local History Studies' (pp. 137-197) are not indexed.

Index

Index